MONEY ISN'T THE PROBLEM, YOU ARE

GARY M. DOUGLAS & DR. DAIN HEER

ACCESS
CONSCIOUSNESS®
PUBLISHING

ACCESS CONCIOUSNESS PUBLISHING COMPANY, LLC
San Diego, California
www.AccessConsciousnessPublishing.com

Second Edition 2013
Printed in the United States of America
International printing in the U.K. and Australia
First Edition Published by Big Country Publishing 2012

ISBN-13: 978-1-939261-06-9
ISBN-10: 1939261066

Cover Art by: Katarina Wallentin
Cover Image © Alexey Audeev istockphoto
Interior Design by: Anastasia Creatives
Interior Image © Khalus istockphoto

CONTENTS

INTRODUCTION

This book is written for people who live in a constant state of difficulty around money, whether it's spending too much, not having enough, or having too much.

I'm Gary Douglas, the founder of Access, an energy transformation system that provides people with tools they can use to remove their limitations and disabilities and create some pretty amazing and wonderful new possibilities for themselves. In this book, my friend and collaborator, Dain Heer, and I share processes, tools, and points of view about money that you can use to change the way money flows into your life.

This book is based on our Access Money Seminar, which we've taught in cities throughout the United States, Costa Rica, Australia and New Zealand. We started offering a money seminar because we discovered people were always trying to find a solution to what they thought was their money problem.

I've had plenty of so-called money problems myself, and I have done so many courses on money that I went cross-eyed at the idea of taking another money class. In the end, none of the money classes I took ever changed anything about the way I approached money.

I still had the same "money problems" after I completed the course. My relationship to money began to change as Access developed and I discovered fresh points of view that could be used to create a different relationship with money. In this book, Dain and I offer these viewpoints and the philosophies behind them, as well as tools and techniques you can use to handle whatever your money situation is.

Gary Douglas

Santa Barbara

Chapter One

MONEY, MONEY, MONEY

DO YOU HAVE A MONEY ISSUE?

Dain and I have a friend who wanted to make a lot of money.

He said, "I have a money issue."
I said, "No, you don't."
He said, "Yes, I do."
I said, "No, you don't."
Finally he asked, "What do you mean?"
I said, "You don't have a money issue; you're just not willing to receive."
He said, "That's not true."
I said, "Yes, it's true. I'll prove that money is not your issue. I'll give you a million dollars, tax-free, if you go back to where you were before you started Access and stay there."
He said, "No f---ing way."

It's not about money. It never is. It's about what you're willing to receive. If you're willing to receive the freedom of life, then money has no value to you. A lot of people think money is a solution, but it's not.

Money Is Never the Solution

Money is never the solution because money is never the problem. If you try to use money as a solution, you will only create another problem to solve with the money that you have, or the money you don't have.

Is Money Going to Solve Your Problem?

Think about it for a moment. Is money going to solve your problem—or are you? You are. How do you do it? You solve what seems to be a money problem by claiming and owning the truth of you. What do I mean by this?

Many years ago, I was in real estate. I was making over $100,000 a year, and my wife was making over $100,000 a year. We were doing well. We were hot. We were cool. We were in with the rich people. We got invited to the rich people's part of town for parties and events. We were hobnobbing with the socially elite. It was awesome.

Then my business took a nosedive. My income went from over $100,000 a year to $4,000. Of course, it didn't help that our mortgage payments were $5,000 a month, our car payments were in the $1,500 a month category, and our kids were in private schools at $15,000 per kid per year.

We filed every form of bankruptcy known to mankind as we went through the process of losing everything. All of our friends in the rich people part of town no longer wanted to socialize with us.

How odd, because guess what is the one prejudice in the world you cannot overcome? Poverty. No money. If you have plenty of money, it doesn't matter what race, color, creed or religion you are or how crazy you are. You're just fine. I tell people to be as weird as they truly are. Just get rich so you're seen as eccentric, not crazy.

We got to the point where we had no money. Our kids had to quit private school. We lost our cars, lost our house, lost just about everything we owned. I went to work for other companies and I hated it. Nothing was working for me until I finally recognized the only choice I had was to do this crazy, wacky, wild stuff we call Access. And once I started in that direction, everything started to turn around. Isn't that interesting?

When you are unwilling to claim, own and be everything you are, as the outrageous, wonderful being you are—no matter how much you want to resist and react to it, no matter how much you want to get away from it—you bankrupt yourself in every respect until you have no choice.

Are you willing to give up the no-choice point of view and start recognizing that the way to create everything you want is to be as wild and crazy and wacky as you truly are? Stop pretending that you're weak, pale and uninteresting.

People think, *If I were to get rich and I had the money I wanted, I'd stop doing what I'm doing and I'd live a different life.* But it doesn't work that way.

Studies have shown that when people win the lottery, within anywhere from one to two years, they're in exactly the same financial condition they were in before they won. Although it's at a higher level, they have the same degree of debt, they have the same degree of limitation, and they have the same financial mess they had before they won the money. Money, it turns out, is never the solution.

But if you're doing what is true for you, then winning the lottery won't matter. In fact, if you won the lottery tomorrow, it would just give you an opportunity to create more of the great things you already know you can create.

Receiving is the Problem and You Are the Solution

The real "money problem" is that you're not willing to receive you into your life. The biggest thing you're unwilling to receive is how incredibly great you really are. Money is not the problem. Money is not the solution. Receiving is the problem and you are the solution. When you start receiving the greatness of who you truly are, everything in your life starts to change—including your money. If you are willing to receive the greatness of you, and allow the world to see the greatness of you, the world will then gift to you what you truly deserve. The willingness to perceive and receive yourself differently is the beginning of creating what you truly desire in your life. That's the place where you have to start.

So, What's It Going to Take for Me to Show Up in My Life?

At this point, you've got to be frustrated with being told you're great and wonderful. Okay, fine. You know that, and yet you've never been able to achieve what you desire. You might even be pissed off and asking, *So, what's it going to take for me to show up in my life?*

That's a question you need to ask, because the universe will give you an answer if you're willing to ask a question and listen to its reply.

Please keep reading. Throughout the rest of this book are tools, techniques and information you can use to help you show up in your life. We hope you will use them to begin to create the life you would like to have.

DO YOU WANT MONEY?

The natural state of things here on planet Earth, contrary to anything you may have been told, is a state of abundance. If you look around when you are in nature, you'll see that when humans aren't doing their best to destroy things, there's no place where life is not thriving and abundant. There is no place that doesn't abound in plant, animal, bird and insect life. Even in so-called barren landscapes, there's an unimaginable amount of life going on. If you stop using a road, even one paved over with asphalt, in a very short period of time, cracks will appear, weeds will start growing, and pretty soon the road will become completely overgrown and disappear. It's a terrifically abundant universe and it's only when the humans manage to bring in the concrete that we stop experiencing nature's abundance. Only where humans trod do barrenness or poverty exist.

Poverty consciousness is what keeps us from perceiving and experiencing the ongoing natural state of abundance. Poverty consciousness is not a reflection of how things really are: it's a state of mind we create. It's the place we function from when we tell ourselves: *I don't have enough. I never have enough.* No matter what happens, I will never have enough. There are a million variations on the theme: *I just have enough to survive. I don't need more than this amount of money to make it.*

It's the point of view that lack is more real than abundance. It's the idea that it's more noble to be poverty stricken than to be wealthy. Some people actually think it's morally superior to be poor. They have the pride of poverty. Dain tells how people in his family used to say, "At least we have a great family and we're happy. Those people with money aren't happy." He says he'd look around and say to himself, "They couldn't be any more unhappy than you? I don't think so!"

Often people with poverty consciousness take pride in being poverty-stricken. Or they believe they can only be comfortable with people who are at their socio-economic level. They will only be comfortable around people as poor as they are: *I wouldn't be comfortable with rich people, because rich people are different, you know.* Well, okay. Look at the category you've just put yourself into!

Poverty consciousness is not a state of mind that only "poor" people have. Rich people can have it as well. I went to a billionaire's party recently, and it seemed like everyone was trying to be the best at degrading their gardeners and their help. This is what they thought being rich meant: degrading the help. *Oh, it's so hard to get good help.* No, it isn't! It's easy to get good help if you treat people well. Even though they have lots of money, there is an unwillingness to receive the greatness of anyone. They think they have to control their employees and pay them as little as possible. Poverty consciousness is not about the amount of money you have; it's about the way you treat yourself and others, and the abundance you're willing to see in the world.

The word *want* is a key component of poverty consciousness. Do you know what the word *want* means? It means to *lack.* Every time you say *I want,* you're saying *I lack.* If you say, *I want more money,* you'll start to lack more and more all the time. If you start paying attention to what you think or what you say, you'll see exactly how you're creating the abundance — or the lack of it — that's showing up in your life.

Look up want in the dictionary. You might have to find it in an older dictionary; dictionaries that were made prior to 1946 have correct definitions of the words of the English language. After 1946, they started to change definitions to reflect the colloquial usage. If you look at the word *want* in a dictionary published prior to 1946, you'll see there are several definitions of *want* meaning to *lack* and only one that means *to desire. To desire is to look for something to be available in the future.* So, even with that definition, you're still in trouble.

Listen to people who are truly abundant; the word *want* isn't in their vocabulary. They don't know the word. They don't have the idea that *want* is part of life. Everything is about having it, getting it, going for it, and allowing it.

There's an old proverb that says *Waste* not, *want* not. Waste not, lack not. If you recognize that the word *want* means to *lack*, and you listen to yourself, you'll see that you're using it all the time. Ask yourself, *What would it take for the word "want" to fall out of my vocabulary?* Instead of creating from *I want money*, allow yourself to create from *I **don't** want money*, because every time you say, *I want more money*, you're saying, *I lack of it* — and that's exactly what shows up in your life.

Try this: Say, *I don't want money* ten times.

> I don't want money.
> I don't want money.
> I don't want money.
> I don't want money.
> I don't want money.
> I don't want money.
> I don't want money.
> I don't want money.
> I don't want money.
> I don't want money.

What happened? Did saying *I don't want money* make you feel lighter or heavier? *Lighter* refers to a sense of expansion and possibility, and a greater sense of space. (You might have even smiled or laughed out loud.) *Heavier* refers to a feeling of contraction, of things weighted down, and less possibility.

If you're like most people, saying *I don't want money* made you feel lighter. Why is that? It's because the truth always makes you feel lighter. A lie makes you feel heavier. The truth of you is you don't lack of money, and saying so shows you're willing to bring it on. You can create receiving in your life by saying that ten times every morning. When people around you say, *I want money*, you can smile knowingly and say, *I **don't** want money!*

DO YOU WORRY ABOUT MONEY?

Do you ever worry about not having enough money? When was the last time you worried about it? Get the feeling of that. Do you have it? Okay, make that feeling infinite. Make it as big as the universe. Make that feeling bigger than the universe. Not eternal, but infinite. You can imagine sticking the needle of a giant air pump into the middle of your worry, and then blowing it up so it's bigger than the universe, but making something bigger than the universe is not really something you have to think about or do. It's just an awareness, and it usually happens as soon as you've asked to do it.

What happens to your money worry when you make it infinite? Does it get fuller and more substantial? Does it have a greater sense of reality? Or does it fade away and disappear? If it goes away, which is what we suspect it will do, then it's a lie. The worry might be something you think is true, but it really isn't. You've bought something that's not true.

Now think about somebody you care about. Make that feeling infinite, bigger than the universe. Does it become more substantial or less substantial? More substantial? Isn't that interesting? When you think about how much you care for someone, and you make it infinite, bigger than the universe, you see it's even bigger than you're willing to admit to yourself. If you were willing to admit how much you care about someone else, and you were truly willing to care that much about yourself, how much do you think you would be willing to receive?

When you take the caring that you have, and you make it infinite, it becomes fuller and more present. It occupies more space than the upset did. You realize that you care more than you acknowledge. You may say, "Yeah, yeah, I care," but when you fill it out and make it substantial, you can see how very much you care. It's almost as if we are afraid to care that much.

Think About Having Plenty of Money

Now, think about having plenty of money. Get the feeling of having plenty of money. Make it infinite, bigger than the universe. Does it get more substantial or less? More substantial? And when you think about not having money, when you say, *Oh no, I'm broke, I can't do this,* if you make those feelings or worries infinite, bigger than the universe, what happens to them? They go away.

If You Create Based on a Lie, Can You Create a Truth Out of It?

Isn't this interesting? We tend to buy into lies like *I don't have any money,* and then we try to create our lives based on those lies. If you attempt to create based on a lie, can you create a truth out of it? No way. If you lie to yourself or buy into false points of view, you create limitations that do not allow you to expand into what is possible with money.

Sometimes Dain tells stories about one side of his family that thought they were lucky if they had enough money to put food on the table. His grandparents had grown up during the depression and there were times when they didn't have food. Their point of view was they were successful if they had enough money to buy food. Dain bought that point of view as a truth, and held on to it until he started Access. He bought the idea that having enough money to have food on the table was a measure of success. Once he started Access, he realized, "Wait a minute! That's not true!"

Shortly after he got started in Access and was seeing some different possibilities in life, we drove up to San Francisco together to do an Access course. We were going to be there for three days and Dain brought ten peanut butter and jelly sandwiches, three pounds of trail mix and three boxes of granola bars. Since he didn't have any money, he thought that would be the food he'd eat while he was there.

At one point during the drive, I put a piece of Big Red gum in my mouth, chewed it for about ten minutes, spat it out and put another piece in. I chewed that one for ten minutes, spat it out and put another one in. I chewed that one for twenty minutes and put a new piece in. Dain wasn't saying anything, but he was freaking out every time I put a new piece of gum into my mouth.

> Finally he asked, "Why do you do that?"
> I said, "Do what?"
> He said, "Chew one piece of gum after the other like that."
> I said, "Because I only like the taste at the beginning! After that it's boring."

Dain came from a family where you chewed your gum for a day and a half. He had never considered the possibility you could do anything so extravagant with a dollar pack of gum. He'd never considered a different standard of affluence for himself. It busted his whole paradigm of not having enough. His reaction was, "Wait a minute! You can do that?"

Most of us buy into lies and limitations like this as we're growing up. *This is what success is, or This is what I can (or can't) have.* In Dain's case the lie was, *Abundance is being able to feed yourself.* That was his family's point of view, and that's the point of view he bought. Is that what abundance is? No, of course not. When he saw that he'd been trying to create his financial life around a lie, new possibilities started to appear.

Instead of making yourself nuts about money—which is something that we're all very good at, by the way—instead of worrying about money, or living in a state of near-poverty, start to realize that your worries, concerns and beliefs about money are not real. And when you realize they're not real, you won't buy into them and you won't create your life based on what is not real or true.

Make It Bigger Than the Universe

Use this exercise to get at the truth of issues. When you make things bigger than the universe, what is true becomes more full and substantial—it feels more real, it takes up more space, and what's a lie dissipates. It goes away. Change what happens with money in your life by using this simple tool—and create from what's true for you.

I CAN'T AFFORD IT

Have you ever told yourself, *I can't afford this?* Years ago I was working at an antique shop rearranging furniture for them. They hired me because every time I rearranged things, something they had in stock for two years would sell. They'd have me come in and do a rearrangement about every two weeks.

I was making $37.50 an hour, which was pretty good money at that time. I was doing that along with everything else I could to support my kids and my wife. The shop owners were so happy with what I was doing they said, "You know what? Anything you want to buy at the store, we'll give it to you at our cost and you can put it on terminal layaway. You can have it whenever you can get it paid off. Just keep working for us."

This was not a low-end antique shop. This was a place that had $20,000 bedroom sets. They had diamond rings that were $35,000. I looked at them and said, "Who can afford this stuff?" After they said that to me, I looked around the shop, and suddenly I realized I could have anything in it.

It's What We Think We Can't Have
That Becomes Valuable

Once I recognized that I could afford anything I wanted—it might take me a while to take it home, but I could afford to have anything in there—I realized none of it mattered to me. I didn't care anymore. It's what we think we can't afford or what we think we can't have that becomes valuable. It becomes valuable, not because it has true value, but because we can't have it. We make the scarcity the significance. So every time you say, *I can't afford it*, you're saying you're not worth it. *I can't afford it* means *I can't have it*. How many times have you decided you couldn't afford an item and settled for something that was less than what you wished to have? You can afford anything. Almost any shop in the world will do layaway for you.

Dain and I recently went into a pawnshop. They had a sign, "Lay Away Now." The whole idea was you could go into this shop—they had stuff in there for up to $20,000—and they would let you put anything on layaway. If you put it on time payments, you could have anything in there. But the question is, do you really want it?

What Would I Really Like to Have?

Practice this on your own. Go into a store and walk around saying, *Okay, I can have anything here I truly desire. What would I really like to have?* You'll look at things and say, *No. No. That's nice. That's nice. That's nice.* And you'll walk out saying, *You know what? There's nothing in there I truly would like to have.*

I'm Going to Have This in My Life

If you do find something you'd like to have, say, *I'm going to have this in my life*, and walk out without looking at the price tag. Why don't you look at the price tag? Because if you do, you're creating a limitation about what it's going to cost and how you can't afford it. If you don't look at the price tag and you just say, *I'm going to have this in my life*, then you can create an opportunity for the universe to drop it into your lap in some way you never imagined possible, at a price you're willing to pay.

> Recently my daughter said, "I'd like to have a Gucci wallet, Dad. They're $250."
> I said, "Okay, that's good. We'll see what can happen."

Three weeks later I stopped at a garage sale for no apparent reason and there was a Gucci wallet for sale. It was three dollars. I assumed it had to be a knockoff and took it home. Turns out it was the real thing.

IF MONEY WEREN'T THE ISSUE, WHAT WOULD YOU CHOOSE?

When you are shopping for an item, you can take away the sense of *need* and the sense of *no money* by asking yourself, *If money weren't the issue, what would I choose?* Most of us make choices based on what we think we need—and can't have. When you ask yourself, *If money weren't the issue, what would I choose?*, it removes money as the basis of your choice.

Dain went to buy a printer. He was looking at several different models, and I asked, "If money weren't the issue, which one would you choose?"

His first thought was, "Oh, I'd pick the biggest one!" It was $500, which was a little out of his range, but that's what he thought he would get if money weren't the issue. But then he started looking around, and he found another printer that did almost everything the $500 one did. It was $150. He said, "Oh, if money weren't the issue, I'd choose the $150 printer." Once he got rid of the *I need this but I can't have it*, he saw he could have everything he desired at a much better price.

Like Dain, most of us assume that if money weren't the issue, we'd buy the best and most expensive item. When you remove money as the issue, you can see, *Oh, I don't really want the big one*. Sometimes the best is not really what you need. For $150 you get everything you wanted in the first place.

Rather than assuming that if you had the so-called *best* you would do more, have more and create more, you can use this question to give you a sense of what your personal perspective is. It allows you to see what the true value of something is — for you. It snaps you out of the viewpoint *I can't have this because . . .* If your personal choice were the only criterion for choosing, what would you choose? You'd get the best for you, given the circumstances for which you're buying things.

There are also times when you'll ask, *If money weren't the issue, what would I choose?*, and you'll decide to get the most expensive thing — again, because you're not making money the criterion. You're making a choice based on what's best for you.

ARE YOU WILLING TO PAY TAXES?

Some people resist paying taxes. They have decided they never want to pay taxes again, and they'll do whatever they can to avoid it. But that is a very bad decision, because when they do this, they cut down the money they're willing to receive.

In order to have, you must be willing to receive everything, including taxation. If you're not willing to pay taxes, then you're not willing to have the income. Personally, I'd like to pay more taxes. You want to be able to pay outrageous amounts of taxes because that means you can receive outrageous amounts of money.

We worked with a man who joined an un-taxing group, which held the position that it is illegal for the IRS to collect taxes. Their viewpoint is that the IRS is a private corporation that has been given the tax collecting system and it is not covered in the Constitution, so therefore they are an illegal group.

> After he told us about this, I said, "Cool. Let me tell you something about your income. Since you joined the group it's dropped by half."
> The guy said, "Whoa, how did you know that?"
> I said, "Because you're trying to hide from the government. When you try to hide, it means you're not allowing yourself to receive. It's impossible to stay hidden and also increase the amount of money you're making."

Is there some part of your life you are hiding? Everything you are trying to hide with regard to taxes and taxation, and all that kind of thing, would you destroy and uncreate all of those decisions, and claim and own that you can pay whatever friggin' tax you choose? The best defense is always to be offensively rich.

DEBT vs. PAST EXPENDITURES

Sometimes people ask me about debt, and where debt fits into all this talk about money. Have you ever noticed that *debt* sounds very much like *death*? Did you know that the word *mortgage* comes from *mort*, meaning *death*, and that it originally meant *dead pledge* or to the death of it? In other words, *I am going to work for this house until I am dead*, which is pretty much the way most people do it.

When you have debts to pay, instead of thinking of yourself as a debtor—and we've all had many lifetimes in which debtor prisons actually existed and we went to jail for owing money—think about what you are paying off as past expenditures. You have past expenditures to pay off—not debts.

If you function from the point of view of *past expenditure* rather than *debt*, you will start to clear that stuff. Every time you say *debt*, you trigger all the remembrances of all the lifetimes you went to debtor's prison. Let's get rid of debt.

CREDIT

If you have credit then you can be in debt. Isn't that great? Have you worked to make yourself creditworthy so you could have a bigger debt? That's the way it works. If you aren't creditworthy, you aren't debtworthy. Creditworthy means you can owe more money. How cool is that?

We suggest you change your perspective about credit. Don't try to create creditworthiness. Look for the abundance of your cashworthiness. Ask: *How do I increase the flow of cash? What are the infinite possibilities for a whole hell of a lot of cash to come into my life?*

> I have people say to me, "Oh, I have all this debt."
> I say, "Okay, so you've got all this debt. How much more would you have to earn per month in order to pay it off?"
> They say, "I have no idea. My monthly credit card payments are $500."
> I say, "Great. That means in twenty years you'll have that sucker paid off."

If you pay the smallest amount of money that's owed on your credit card, do you realize the $40 dinner you just charged will end up costing you $200? Gee, I wonder why banks like you to charge things. It's good to charge, right? Get over it. It's good to make money. That's what's good.

Are you more interested in how cool it is to have credit cards than how cool it is to make money?

> Sometimes I see people open their wallets and a long line of credit cards fall out, and I ask, "Why do you need those?"

They say, "Well, I have lots of credit. Look at all the things I can buy."

I say, "You can't buy shit. You don't have any money."

They say, "Yes, but I can buy lots of things."

I say, "Yeah, but you don't have any money. Are you stupid and insane?"

I know someone who went through his wallet and took out all of his credit cards and put them away so that he wasn't carrying his debt around with him. Great idea. Then he said when he gets all the cards paid off, he can slowly but surely put them back into his wallet — if he's foolish enough to do that.

If you can start to live with the cash and the money that flows in your life, you'll start to expand. When we think, *Oh my God, I'm out of money*, that's just a point of view. *I'm out of money. I've got to use my credit card.* That point of view, all by itself, is enough to lock you up, because it's a lie.

Give up the credit cards. Find a different way. Create money. Don't create credit and the debt that follows it. The tools that follow will help you do this.

TITHE TO THE CHURCH OF YOU

A tithe is a tenth part of one's income that is contributed to charity or to support one's church. Do you believe in tithing to your church? What about tithing to the Church of You? Would you be willing to do that?

Here is what you do: You take 10 percent of everything that comes into your life and you put it away. Put it into a savings account. Put it in the bank. Put it under the mattress. It doesn't matter where you put it, just put it away. Don't spend it.

If you continue to put that 10 percent away, you demonstrate to the universe that you desire money. When you tithe to the Church of You, the universe responds: *Oh, you like money? Okay, we'll* give *you more money.* You might be thinking, *Gosh, I can barely make* ends meet now. How am I going to set aside 10 percent? The answer is: by doing it. The universe honors whatever you request of it. If you honor you by tithing 10 percent of what you take in, the universe says, *Oh, you want to be honored with 10 percent? Here's some more to honor yourself with.*

Do you take care of your bills before you tithe to yourself? When you pay your bills first, have you noticed how the number of bills grows? Why is that? You're honoring your bills and the universe says, *Oh, you like bills? Okay, we'll give you more bills.*

This doesn't mean you don't pay your bills. What you do is honor you, and if you have to stretch things a little bit or play catch-up later, no problem. If you start to honor yourself first and tithe 10 percent to the Church of You, within six months to a year your whole financial situation will turn around. You will hit financial targets you made a billion years ago when you said, *When I have this amount of money, I'm going to be rich. When I hit this amount of money, I'm very rich.* These are decisions that you don't even remember making, but when you achieve them, you experience a sense of peace within yourself and the frantic need for money goes away.

Just 10 Percent

My friend who owned the antique shop was borrowing $100,000 every six months to go to Europe and buy antiques. The bank charged him ten points up front to get the money. That means they charged him $10,000 to borrow the money. So he got $90,000 but he had to pay back $100,000 plus they charged him 15 percent interest on the money. So if he took a year to pay it off, how much money was he paying? What was the interest rate? Twenty-five percent. It cost him $25,000 to borrow $100,000 if he didn't pay it back within six months.

He was working his ass off. One day I said to him, "If you would put 10 percent away, within six months to a year your whole financial condition will have turned around."

He started doing it and within six months he had doubled the size of his shop and was going to Europe to buy antiques with his own $100,000. His business doubled, and his wife's business went from $250,000 a year to $1.5 million.

> About two years later I walked into his shop, looked around, and I said, "You used the 10 percent, didn't you?"
> He said, "Oh, you are psychic."
> I said, "Yeah, that and the fact that I can feel the energy in here. You're desperate to sell things. It no longer feels like a place where everything is worth a lot. It's like everything is on discount. You've changed the energy of your shop and you expect to succeed based on what?"

Since then he's gotten more and more desperate because he didn't go back to tithing 10 percent. Does he return my calls anymore? No. Why? He knows that if he went back to doing the 10 percent it would work again, but he won't do it. His choice.

Carry Cash

If you carry your money around in your pocket and don't spend it, it makes you feel wealthy. What will then show up in your life is more and more money, because you're telling the universe you're abundant. Decide upon a sum of money that you, as a rich person, will always carry with you. Whatever that amount would be — $500, $1,000, $1,500 — carry it with you in your wallet at all times. We don't mean carry a gold credit card. That doesn't cut it. You've got to carry cash in your pocket, because it's about recognizing the wealth of you.

You can turn your cash into gold coins if you like gold coins. You can trade it in for diamonds if you like. Keep it in some form of currency that you can transport easily. I wouldn't convert my cash into tankers full of oil if I were you. They can sink.

When we tell you to set 10 percent aside, we're not talking about putting this money into investments or projects. We want you to be like Scrooge McDuck. Do you remember him? He was Donald Duck's billionaire uncle. He loved money! He would fill his swimming pool with dollar bills and dive into it. Do you want to have lots of money? Then be willing to have it for real. Have lots of money hanging around.

Carry this amount of money with you. It can be part of your 10 percent if you wish. Keep it with you at all times and don't spend it. When you know you have $500, $1,000, or $1,500 in your pocket, you say, *Hey, I'm cool!* You walk tall. You know that you can walk into any place and buy anything there—but you don't have a need for it.

Need vs. Greed

When you have a sense of need, it always leads to a sense of greed, which means you will try to hold on to what you have as though there's never going to be any more. When you have a sense of that nice, fat amount of money in your pocket and the possibility of things growing, all kinds of changes can occur for you, because you're not functioning from the point of view that you have a limited amount. You start to function from the point of view, *I've got money in my pocket. I've got thousands of dollars in my drawer at home. I play with money. I throw it on the bed and I roll on it naked because it feels really good.*

Have you ever actually looked at your money? What does it look like? Whose picture is on a hundred dollar bill? We know because we carry lots of them. They're pretty. That's right, they're pretty and we carry them in our pockets. We like all those dollars. They're cute. If you changed your mind and thought money was cute and you loved the way it looked, maybe you could receive it more easily.

Chapter Two

SOME COOL TOOLS

FROM PERSPIRATION TO INSPIRATION

In Access we don't look for the cutting edge of things. We look for the creative edge, because if you're constantly creating your life, then you're expanding it.

In this section, we offer some questions, techniques and tools that will give you the opportunity to go from perspiration to inspiration in creating the life you would like to have. But here's the deal: If you want your life to change, you have to use them.

These are the most simple, dynamic tools you can imagine, but 90 percent of the people we share them with never use them. You, too, may refuse. If you're addicted to unconsciousness around money, you won't do what it takes to change your life.

You'll read through this book and say, "I spent all that money on that money book and nothing has changed. It was worthless."

Well, it is worthless if you don't use it. But if you're determined to make some changes in your life and create a different reality around money—and everything else—we invite you to try these tools.

LIVE IN THE QUESTION

The universe is an infinite place and it has infinite answers. When you ask an unlimited question, the universe will give you the answer. But what we usually do is ask a limited question like, *How do I get from Point A to Point B?* And when we do that, the mind goes to work, trying to figure it out: Do *this, this,* this and this.

When you try to work out the way you're going to make something happen, you are figuring out the answer rather than asking a question. Don't try to figure it out. You'll limit yourself. Your mind is a dangerous thing. It can only define what you already know. It cannot be infinite and unlimited. Whenever you have an answer, that's the sum total of what can show up for you. But when you live in the question, infinite possibilities are available. Try some of these questions and see what happens.

What Would It Take for ___ to Show Up?

When you live in the question, you create an invitation. When you ask, *What would it take for _____ to show up?*, the universe will give you opportunities for that to happen.

You get stuck in your life and think, *It's either this—or this. I can do this—I can't do this. I can be this—I can't be this. The only way I can ___ is if Joe lends me $5,000. I could never afford a ____. I just don't have the money to ____.* These are limited points of view. Adopt an unlimited point of view with the question, *What would it take for ___ to show up?*

Recently I went to take some money out of my savings account because I didn't seem to have enough money. I was saying, "Damn it! Why don't I have enough money? I don't understand this! What's it going to take for more money to show up? It's ridiculous that I don't have enough money. What's it going to take?"

The next day, I got my briefcase, which I hadn't used for about three months, out of the closet, and there was $1,600 in cash that I had stowed there for some reason. Two days after that, Dain and I flew to Florida and when we got there, our friend Jill handed Dain an envelope and said, "This was with the credit card machine."

Dain asked, "What's this?"
She said, "Checks that were never cashed from a class you and Gary did."
There was $2,000 worth of checks in it.

The same day I got a call from a lady whose credit card hadn't been charged for $1,800 worth of services, and a day later, I found a check for $500 in a drawer where I'd left it.

That was the $6,000 I'd taken out of my savings account. I said, "Hmm. I guess I wasn't short of money. I just wasn't looking."

The funny thing is, it's still happening. I had a lady call me today and say, "You know that class I took a couple of months ago? They didn't charge my account for it. I'm mailing you a check."

I said, "Okay, cool! How does it get any better than this?"

You have to ask a question for the universe to give you an answer. You have to ask. It's no good to say, *I want more money.* That only means *I lack of more money*—and there's no question in it. Always use a question: *What would it take for ____ to show up?*

What's Right About This That I'm Not Getting?

Another great question is, *What's right about this that I'm not getting?* Are there areas in your life where you think you only have the choice of either/or? Do you think you have to choose one side of the coin or the other, rather than having the infinite capacity to do anything? Are you seeing yourself as a tiny speck in the universe and asking, *What's wrong with me?*

What does that do to you? It puts you in the finite. You don't become the unlimited being you really are and you eliminate possibilities for change. Instead of asking, *What's wrong with me?* ask, *What's right about this I'm not getting?*

When Dain and I first started to work together, he lived with my ex-wife and me. After a while, he found a place to live on his own, and I was helping him move. As we were delivering the last load of his stuff, the owner of the place appeared and went ballistic. She said things like, "You can't move in here. You get out! I didn't agree to this. You can't have this place."

> Dain withered and asked, "What's wrong with me that I can't make this work?"
> I said, "Wrong question, dude. What's right about this you're not getting?"

Well, it turned out that the owner of the place, who lived on the property, talked non-stop and was completely nuts. Instead of living there, he got a far nicer two-bedroom apartment overlooking a park in a really nice area of town, and he didn't have to rent an office and was able to work out of his home.

Everything turned out way better than what he had set up, because when it fell apart, he was willing to ask, "What's right about this I'm not getting?"

You as a being would not do anything wrong—you just wouldn't. But there might be something right about the situation you're not getting. How do you discover what that is? Ask, *What's right about this I'm not getting?* Whatever it is, the question asks for the awareness and unlimited capacity to perceive and look. Use this question to unlock possibilities for change in your life

How Does It Get Any Better Than This?

Here is a question to use on a daily basis. When you use it in a bad situation, you get clarity on how to change things, and when you use it in a good situation, all kinds of interesting things can show up.

In New York, a lady walked out of an Access class and found a dime in front of the elevator. She said, "Oh, how does it get any better than this?", and stuck it in her pocket. She walked downstairs and out onto the street, saw a ten-dollar bill on the ground, stuck it in her pocket and asked, "How does it get any better than this?" She was on her way to the subway but waved down a cab instead and rode to the front of her building. As she stepped out, she saw something glittering in the gutter. She reached down and picked up a diamond bracelet. At this point she said, "It can't get any better than this," which was a big mistake. When you say that, that's all there is. Otherwise, who knows, she might have owned the Empire State Building by now.

I'm not guaranteeing that you're going to turn a dime into diamonds, but you can never tell what is going to happen. Just keep asking, *How does it get any better than this?*

PERCEIVE, KNOW, BE AND RECEIVE

Do you want to know what's going to make your job better or how to improve your money situation, or your business, or your relationship? In any area of your life that is not working for you, there is something you are not perceiving, not knowing, not being or not receiving.

How can we say this? It's because we know you are an infinite being. As an infinite being, you have the infinite capacity to perceive, know, be and receive. This means that in order to create your life as the limitation it has become, there have to be things that you are unwilling to perceive, know, be and receive.

Say the following thirty times a day for three days: *Perceive, know, be and receive what I refuse, dare not, must never and must also perceive, know, be and receive that will allow me total clarity and ease with _____.* Or you can use a simplified version: *What must I perceive, know, be and receive that would allow me to ____?*

You can put anything in the blank. This question starts to unlock where you're not showing up.

If you will do this thirty times a day for three days, somewhere at the end of the third day or into the fourth day, you'll start to have an inspired way of looking at things. Suddenly you'll ask, *Why didn't I think of that before?* You couldn't think of it before because you refused, or you dared not, or you thought that you must never perceive or receive something, or you thought you had to perceive or receive something in order to get there.

This simple question will help you unlock your limitations. *Perceive, know, be and receive what I refuse, dare not, must never and must also perceive, know, be and receive that will allow me total clarity and ease with _____.* Thirty times a day will begin to change whatever area of your life is not working the way you would like it to work.

YOU'VE GOT TEN SECONDS TO LIVE
THE REST OF YOUR LIFE

You've got ten seconds to live the rest of your life. The world is filled with lions, tigers, bears and poisonous snakes. They're going to eat you. You've got ten seconds. What are you going to choose?

If you do everything in your life in ten-second increments, you will find you cannot make a wrong decision. If you do anger for ten seconds and get over it, you'll make no wrong choices. If you love for ten seconds, you can love anyone and everyone for that amount of time, no matter who they are. You can hate someone for ten seconds. You can divorce your spouse for ten seconds. And you can love him or her in the next ten.

If you live in ten-second increments, you will create being in the present moment. Most people, rather than living in the moment, keep trying to create a plan and a system for the future so it will show up the way they want it. But there's only one place we can live and that's right here, right now. Anything else kills you. You don't get to have a life. You miss out on your own life.

People have asked, "How can you do business in ten-second increments?" In ten seconds, you can decide whether you wish to talk to that person or not. You can know whether he or she is available. You can know. Ten-second increments force you to stop thinking and to go into knowing.

In ten seconds you can start to break down the conditioning that has you figuring things out and planning in advance. You can learn how to choose and how to be present. You can't judge in ten seconds because it's here and it's gone. We prolong our agony in life by judging ourselves and trying to fix what we have judged. But what if you just said, *Oh, well, I did that for ten seconds, now what would I like to choose?*

When you do something that you think is bad, how long do you punish yourself for it? How long do you obsess about it? Days? Weeks? Months? Years? If you're living in ten-second increments, you can't do that. Of course, you can't remember anything, either. But that's the good news.

If you practice the art of choosing your life in ten-second increments you will begin to create choice and the opportunity to receive money. Most of us create based on obligation. We say, *Well, I've got to go do this, and I've got to do this, and I've got to do this.* But are those things we'd truly like to do? Usually not, but we keep choosing them. Why? Because we think we have to. We think we're obligated to do them and that if we don't, nobody will pay us. We buy the idea that everybody else is more important than we are. If you had ten seconds to choose the rest of your life, what would you choose?

Would you choose poverty? It's just a choice, neither stupid nor insane. When you live in ten-second increments, you get to choose again. You don't have to stay stuck in poverty.

You've got ten seconds, what do you choose? Wealth? Okay, those ten seconds are over. You've got ten seconds to live the rest of your life, what do you choose? Laughter? Joy? Consciousness?

DESTROY AND UNCREATE YOUR LIFE

One of the things you want to do is to start every day anew. You want to create your life every day. This means that every morning, you need to destroy and uncreate everything you were yesterday. If you have a business, you destroy and uncreate it every morning. If you destroy and uncreate everything in your financial situation every day, you will start to create more money. You will create today. That's part of living in ten-second increments. When you live in the moment, you're not trying to prove your past decision was a right one; you are creating your life moment-by-moment all the time.

We tend to think, *Okay, I've created this beautiful pile of shit over there, so I don't want to uncreate it. I'll just ignore it and walk over here and now I'm going to create something else.* The thing is, the pile of shit is still sitting there and each day you ignore it, it smells stronger and stronger until finally it's overwhelming and you have to deal with it.

Destroy and Uncreate Your Relationship

If you have a relationship and you destroy and uncreate it every day, you will create it anew each day. It keeps you on the creative edge of things. We worked with a couple that had been married twenty-six years, and on their twenty-seventh wedding anniversary, instead of having a new ceremony, they decided to totally destroy and uncreate their relationship. They've been doing it ever since, and they say that the sex keeps getting better and better — and they are having more of it.

Their seventeen-year-old daughter said, "Will you two stop acting like horny teenagers? You're disgusting. You want to do it all the time." This is after being married twenty-seven years. But that's what happens. When you destroy and uncreate everything you have created, what shows up is the opportunity to create something totally new.

Something interesting and unexpected happened when I decided to destroy and uncreate my relationship with my children. My youngest son was always late. You could guarantee that he would be between half an hour to an hour late for absolutely everything. Three days after I destroyed and uncreated my relationship with him, he called and said, "Hey, Dad, can we have breakfast together?"

> I said, "Sure, son, when do you want to do it?"
> He said, "About twenty minutes."
> I said, "Okay, fine."
> I was with Dain, and I said, "We've got at least forty minutes." So we dawdled around for about forty-five minutes.

When we got to the place where we were going to eat, my son was standing on the corner tapping his toe the way I did when he was late. He said, "Where have you been? I've been here for twenty minutes waiting for you!"

> I thought, "Oh my God! The Pod People came and got him during the middle of the night. This is not my son. He's never on time!"

Ever since then, he's been on time. It is friggin' weird. After I destroyed and uncreated my relationship with him, he stopped being late.

Destroying and uncreating does not mean you have to physically destroy anything. It doesn't mean you have to actually end your relationship. What you destroy and uncreate is everything you decided, so you have a greater clarity about what is possible. You destroy and uncreate your decisions and judgments, your obligations, upsets and intrigues, your projections and expectations, and all the things you've decided are going to happen in the future.

How Do You Do This?

How do you do this? You say, *Everything I was yesterday, I now destroy and uncreate.* You can destroy and uncreate anything. You can say, *Everything my relationship was yesterday (or my business, or my financial situation), I now destroy and uncreate.*

What Else Is Possible?

Remember what it was like when you were a kid? Did you start out every day thinking about what you were obligated to do? Or did you want to have fun and play? If you destroy and uncreate your life every day, you can get out of bed every morning with the question, *Okay, so what kind of possibilities can I create today?* Or, *Hey, what else is possible?* If you do this, you will create a whole different reality. You'll be creating with the enthusiasm of youth, because you are no longer who you were yesterday.

Who Am I Today and What Grand and Glorious Adventure Am I Going to Have?

Another question you can use, after you've destroyed and uncreated your life is, *Who am I today and what grand and glorious adventure am I going to have?* If you have destroyed and uncreated yesterday, then you begin to create life as an adventure instead of an obligation.

TRUTH AND LIES

The truth always makes you feel lighter. A lie always makes you feel heavier.

If something makes you feel heavy, it's a lie for you, whether or not it is for anybody else. Don't give your power away to anybody by saying that they know more than you do. You are the source.

Wherever your attention gets stuck on something, you have a truth with a lie attached. Ask: *What part of this is true and what part is a lie, spoken or unspoken?*

What Part Is True?

The majority of lies that stick our attention are unspoken lies. You keep thinking about it. If a thought keeps coming back, ask, *What part is true?*, and the answer will make you feel lighter.

What's the Lie, Spoken or Unspoken, That's Attached to It?

Then ask, *What's the lie, spoken or unspoken, that's attached to it?* When you spot the lie, the whole thing turns loose. It becomes truth and you're free of it.

I had a friend who was a magical healer. He could do miracles just giving you a massage. He could heal your body. He did the Access Foundation and Access I Class, and then said he couldn't afford to do the II and III Class. I said, "I'll give you the classes because you're such a good friend and I really want you to have them."

He said, "Great," but he didn't show up for the classes.
I called him a number of times, but he didn't call me back.

After about two weeks, I was feeling strange about this situation and I went to his wife's office and he was there.

I said, "Hey, can we go for a walk?"
He said, "Okay."
I said, "So, what's the deal that you didn't come to the class?"
He said, "Well, I was thinking about it and I realized that my calling is to sell vitamins."

Sell vitamins? That is his calling? I thought, *That does not make me feel lighter. What's the truth here?* I didn't challenge him, but I wondered, *You just got a $1,400 class offered to you for free and you turned it down. What's going on?* I went away and I was confused. I kept thinking about it.

The Truth Is . . .

A couple days later, I said, *Wait a minute! The truth is he didn't do the class.*

The Spoken Lie

Then I spotted the spoken lie, which was that he wanted to sell vitamins.

The Unspoken Lie

Then I got the unspoken lie, which was that it was *his choice* not to do the class. In truth, it was *his wife* who didn't want him to do it. I got that his wife is the power in the family and she doesn't want him to have any, because that means he might leave her. He was younger, he was good looking, and she didn't get that he loved her for her. She thought he stayed with her because she made the majority of the money, and she decided it was better to keep him powerless.

Once I spotted that, I knew what was going on and I never thought about it again.

Use this with recurring thoughts. Ask yourself, *What part is true?* The answer will make you feel lighter. Then ask, *What's the lie, spoken or unspoken, that's attached to it?* More often the lie that hangs you up is an unspoken lie. Spot the lie and you're free of it.

INTERESTING POINT OF VIEW

When you are in a place of no judgment, you recognize that you are everything and you judge nothing, including yourself. There is simply no judgment in your universe. There is total allowance of all things.

When you are in allowance, you are a rock in the stream. Thoughts, ideas, beliefs, attitudes and emotions come at you, and they go around you and you are still the rock in the stream. Everything is an interesting point of view.

Acceptance is different from allowance. If you are in acceptance, when thoughts, ideas, beliefs and attitudes come at you and you are in the stream, you get washed away. In acceptance, you either align and agree, which is the positive polarity, or you resist and react, which is the negative polarity. Either way, you become part of the stream and you get washed away.

If you are in allowance of what I'm saying, you can say, *Well, that's an interesting point of view. I wonder if there's any truth in that.* You go into a question instead of a reaction. When you go into resistance and reaction or alignment and agreement with points of view, you create limitation. The unlimited approach is, *Interesting point of view.*

How is this in everyday life? You and your friend are walking down the street and he says to you, "I'm broke." What do you do?

> "Oh, you poor thing!" is alignment and agreement.
> "You are!" is resistance and reaction. You know he's going to hit you up for a loan.
> Interesting point of view is, "Really?"

Does someone irritate you? He or she is not the problem. You are. As long as you have any irritation, you've got a problem. Lock yourself in the bathroom and say or think, *Interesting point of view, I have this point of view*, for every point of view you have about them until you get over it and can be in allowance. Then you're free.

It's not about the way others respond to you. It's about your being in allowance of them as completely batshit as they are. You have to be in allowance of where the other person sits in order for them to be able to change.

You don't have to align and agree and love them, nor do you have to resist and react and hate them. Neither of those is real. You simply allow and honor and respect their point of view without buying it. Being in allowance of somebody doesn't mean you have to be a doormat. You just have to be what is.

The hardest thing is to be in allowance with yourself. We tend to judge and judge and judge ourselves. We get locked into trying to be a good parent or a good partner or a good whatever and we're always judging ourselves. But we can be in allowance of our own point of view. We can say, *I had that point of view. Interesting. I did that. Interesting.*

When you're in allowance, everything bcomes an interesting point of view. You do not accept it; you do not resist it. It just is. Life gets easier and easier.

ALL OF LIFE COMES TO ME WITH EASE AND JOY AND GLORY

Our mantra in Access is: All of life comes to me with ease and joy and glory. It's not an affirmation because it's not about having only the positive. It includes the good, the bad and the ugly. We'll take it all with ease and joy and glory. None of it has to be painful, suffering and gory, even though that's the way most of us live our lives. You can have fun instead. What if the purpose of life was merely to have fun? All of life comes to me with ease and joy and glory.

Say it ten times in the morning and ten times in the evening and it will change your life. Put it on your bathroom mirror. Tell your mate the reason it's up there is because you have to remember it. It will change your mate's life as well, just because he or she has to look at it.

Guess What? We're Getting Married!

A lady called me and said, "I want my boyfriend to marry me. How can I get that to happen?"

> I said, "Honey, I'm a psychic, not a wizard. The only thing I can suggest is that you put All of life comes to me with ease and joy and glory up on the mirror where he shaves every morning, and who knows?"
> Three weeks later, she called and said, "Guess what? We're getting married!"

Grandma, What's That?

A grandmother who does Access in New Zealand told us that her grandson saw All of life comes to me with ease and joy and glory on her refrigerator, and he said, "Grandma, what's that? Can I use it?"

She said, "Well, it comes from Access and you can use it—just let people know where it came from."

The grandson, who is the manager of a refrigeration company, had his salesmen say it together ten times every morning, and in eight weeks their sales went from $20,000 to $60,000 per month. That's without changing anything else.

The grandson told his lowest-performing salesman about using, *How does it get any better than this?* The guy started saying it every time he made out a new sales receipt, and his sales went from $7,000 to $20,000 per month.

These people hadn't ever heard of Access and had no idea where these tools came from, but they *used* them—and experienced big changes in the way money flowed into their lives. So can you.

Chapter Three

GET THE VISION OF WHAT YOU WANT YOUR JOB TO BE

DO YOU LIKE YOUR JOB?

Most people, when they take a job, decide they have to accept whatever the employer gives out. They think that if their employer treats them badly, they have to take it. That's the way it's set up. If they don't like it they can leave. Most people choose to stick with their jobs even when they don't like them, because they figure if they are lucky enough to have a job, they'd better hold onto it. They might not get another one. Have you ever suffered from this way of thinking? *If I get this job, I'd better hold onto it because I might not get another.* So much for living in the infinite possibilities.

Get the Vision of What You Want Your Job to Be

Instead of taking a job you don't like and putting up with conditions that make you unhappy, get the vision of what you'd like your job to be.

By vision, we mean more than what it's going to look like. It's the vibration of the components that will bring it to fruition. What would your job feel like? What would be involved in it? How would it show up?

Don't just think it. Get the feeling of it. And when something shows up that feels like that thing, move in that direction. When something doesn't have that feeling, don't go there. If it feels that way a little bit, but it's not the whole thing, don't go there. The moment you take a job so you can survive, survival is all you're ever going to get. Don't succumb to *I have to pay the bills.*

Before I started doing Access, I said, "Okay, I'd like a job where I travel at least two weeks out of the month. I'd like to earn $100,000 minimum a year. I'd like to work with really interesting people and never get bored. I'd like work that's always changing and expanding and getting more fun. I would like a job that, aside from anything else, is about facilitating people in becoming more conscious and more aware of what they'd like to create in their lives.

Those are the things I wanted. I stuck a little bubble of that out in front of me and I pulled energy into it from all over the universe until I felt it growing stronger and then I let little trickles of energy out to all those people who might be looking for me and didn't know it. Every time I encountered something in life that had those aspects to it, or that feeling to it, I did it, whether it made any sense to me or not. I did a lot of different things, but each thing I did led me closer to doing what I am doing today. Anything that felt like what I was asking for, I would do—and that would lead me to the next thing. It was because of this that I ended up with Access. The first thing that shows up may not be the final step, but that's how you choose the things that are your stepping stones.

One day I went to a place where I was asked to do a channeled massage.

> I asked, "What's that? Do I have to keep my eyes open? Do I have to take my clothes off? Do I have to touch your body"? and "Do I get paid?"
> The guy said, "I just want you to do a channeling for my massage therapist."
> I said, "Oh, okay, fine. I can do that."

I did that, and I started using the tools that have become Access. Since then, Access has grown unto itself by word of mouth. Ninety-nine percent of the people who come to it hear about it from a friend and they grab it and they go with it. Why does it grow like that? Because I'm open to it, because I'm willing to receive whatever it is, and because I will step out of my comfort zone and become something else.

What Would a Job that Made Continuous, Increasing Amounts of Money Look Like?

What would a job that made continuous, increasing amounts of money look like or feel like or taste like? What if it wasn't about survival and you didn't even care if you got money for it? What if money wasn't the compelling issue in the process? What if the compelling thing was the ability to achieve what you truly desire in your life? The way you connect to people. The way you help them achieve their desires and goals.

What would you truly like to achieve in your life? That's what you envision. What would it be like to do that? That's the question to ask yourself. Don't ask, *How do I create this?* The *how* creates the need to figure it out, and the need to figure it out creates a limitation.

Ask the Universe to Help

Ask the universe to help you. Say, *Okay, I'd like a job that has this in it — and this — and this — and this.* Start pulling energy into this vision from all over the universe until it feels like it's getting bigger, then let little trickles go out to all those people that are looking for you and don't know it. Every time something that feels like that vision shows up in your life, go for it.

All things are possible. You are an unlimited being. You have unlimited possibilities. Choose what you would like to have in your life.

HOW CAN I USE MY TALENTS AND ABILITIES TO CREATE MONEY?

Many years ago I had an upholstery business, and I discovered I had what turned out to be a unique talent. I could look at a client's carpet or drapes or whatever, and I would know exactly what colors were going to be needed to go with them, and I could keep a clear picture of them in my mind. Six months later I came across some fabric that was exactly the same color as my client's carpet. I called them and told them I'd found just the fabric they needed and they said, "Great. Can you pick it up for us? How many yards do we need for our chair?"

I told them, and I picked up the fabric. Would I charge them for it? No, I wouldn't. Why was that? I didn't recognize this ability as anything special. I figured anybody else could do what I could do, and so it couldn't be worth any money. That's the way it often is with our abilities and talents. They come to us so easily we don't think anything of them. We don't see the value they have to others.

What's the one thing that you do so friggin' easily that it takes no effort? What is so easy for you that you think anybody could do it? Of course, the reality is that nobody else can. You have to start asking yourself, *Okay, what's the talent and ability, the thing that I can do so easily that I think it has no value?* It's that thing—the one you do easily, the thing you think has no value—that is probably the most valuable talent you have. If you start to use it to create money, you'll be amazingly successful.

Back when I worked in real estate, I knew a lady who worked for a big real estate company. She loved cooking. She'd cook amazing meals for her friends and make the most outrageous desserts anybody had ever tasted. Every time she held an open house, she would serve one of her desserts, and every realtor in town would show up.

One day somebody said to her, "You're such a great cook. You ought to open a bakery." She did—and she's a multi-millionaire now. Until someone pointed out to her that she had a unique talent, she thought nothing of it. She just liked to cook. But because somebody finally said, "What you do is great. You ought to create a bakery," she got it. She got out of real estate, where she was making about $100,000 a year, and now she's making millions. She's doing what she loves to do.

Do What You Love To Do

You want to do what you love to do, not what you are passionate about. Do you know where the word *passion* comes from? It comes from the Greek word for *suffering* and *martyrdom;* it was used to refer to Christ's suffering and crucifixion. That's what The Passion means. If you wish to be tacked to the cross, follow your passion. Look at the original definitions of the words you use, because we have a lot of misidentification and misapplication, which means we buy lies about what words mean. It's important to know the true meaning of something. People have told you for years, *Follow your passion.* Has it worked for you? No. There has to be a reason it hasn't worked, and the reason has to do with the definition of the word.

If you've been told that such-and-such is going to create a certain result and it doesn't work, look up the definition in an old dictionary. You may find the root of the word means exactly the opposite of what the person was trying to convey to you. If the energy and the word don't match, there's a misidentification or a misapplication, and that word is misdefined.

If you want to make money, do what you love. If you do what you love, you can make money with it, that is — if you're willing to receive money for love. In other words, you have to be willing to be a prostitute.

But let's get rid of the judgment about being a prostitute. Destroy and uncreate your judgments about being a prostitute, because really, it's when we do something that we *don't* love that we're prostituting ourselves for money.

MAKE A CHOICE TO BE GREATER

We worked with a woman who had a small business, and she decided she wanted to grow it into a larger one. She decided it was not going to be a small business any longer. She went out and hired the most expensive PR firm in her city to promote her business, and almost immediately, she started getting access to large corporations. She was on the radio. An article about her was published in a major executive magazine.

> I asked her what changed, and she said, "I made a choice."
> I asked, "Oh, and what was the choice?"
> She said, "I made a choice to become bigger than I am."

That's what you have to do. You have to make a choice to become bigger than what you've been willing to be.

When I was first promoting and developing Access, I decided that I had to be more outrageous. I had to step up and become more than what I was willing to be. I had to be willing to step out and step up and become controversial. I had to be willing to make a statement that would rock people's worlds in some way.

Once I made that decision, my business started to grow, because I was willing to be more. It's the choice to be more that makes your business grow. It doesn't mean you necessarily have to go out and get a PR firm. There are other ways of doing it.

The important thing is to make the decision, and then the ways of doing it will start to show up in your life. It's when you're unwilling to make a commitment to be bigger than you already are that you get stuck in the same place you've always been and will always be.

I'm talking about the willingness to be more in every respect. You have to stop refusing to be everything you truly are. You've got yourself pretty defined, right? I'm this—I'm this—I'm this. To become more means you have to defy, defeat and destroy those old definitions of yourself.

Just for Today, I Will Be Greater
Than I Was Yesterday

Every morning when you wake up, start out by destroying and uncreating every definition you have of you, and then say, *Just for today, I will be greater than I was yesterday.*

IF YOU'RE GOING TO BE SUCCESSFUL,
WHO DO YOU HAVE TO BE?

Do you think you have to be somebody else in order to be successful? An actor has to become somebody else—but do you? Think about all the identities you have created to supposedly ensure your success. Has this helped you? Or has it made it more difficult for you to have the success you want? Have you actually become lost as to who you are?

If you're going to be successful, who do you have to be? The answer is you have to be yourself. You have to be you. In order to be successful, you have to come out of being lost and claim and own the capacity to show up as you. And you have to destroy everything that does not allow you to perceive, know, be and receive who, what, where, when, why and how you truly are.

What Must I Also Perceive, Know, Be and Receive?

When I was first starting out with Access, I kept asking the question, *What must I also perceive, know, be and receive that would allow me and Access to grow with ease?* I asked that question thirty times a day for about four days. All of a sudden I realized what I wasn't willing to do.

I wasn't willing to be a guru for people. I was not interested in being in control of other people's lives. I was interested in being in control of my own life. I was interested in my life growing. I was not interested in being responsible for anyone else's. The fact that I wasn't willing to appear to be a guru for people who wanted that limited the people who could come into Access.

I discovered I kept trying to prove I wasn't a guru by putting myself down and making myself less than I really was. Once I saw what I was doing, I was willing to say, *Okay, I can appear to be a guru. I can appear to be anything, but I don't have to be it. I can just look that way to others.* I changed that and Access started to grow.

What Must I Also Be?

Then I had to go to a step further. I asked, *So what must I also be?* I realized I had to be controversial. If you're controversial, people talk about you, right? So the good news is I was willing to be as controversial as possible. Once when I was on a radio program in San Francisco talking about a sex and relationship class I was about to give, I said, "And we'll be talking about anal sex and abuse." And the moderator went "Ahem . . . Excuse me, Mr. Douglas . . ." That was fun.

If You're Not Willing to Put Yourself Out There, Can You Receive More?

Because I'm willing to talk about anything, because I'm willing to be utterly outrageous and put myself out there in a way I wasn't willing to before, all kinds of people are showing up to work with me. If you're not willing to put yourself out there, can you receive more? No, you can't. You have to be willing to be controversial if you want to make your life better. You have to be willing to stir the pot. You have to be willing to destroy everything you think is conservative and be out of the control system of your current reality. What would your life be like if you were willing to do that?

The answer is you'd be expansive in your life instead of contractive. Do you look for all the ways you *shouldn't* do things instead of the ways you *could*, or *can*, or *might be able* to do them?

If you're out of control, you won't give a f--- about anybody else's point of view. You won't claim, own and acknowledge rules that do not apply to you. If you're willing to stop living by other people's rules and regulations, then you no longer have to base your life on everybody else's point of view.

What Would Happen If You Were Out of Control?

What would happen if you were out of control, out of definition, out of limitation, out of form, structure, significance, with creating your fabulous, unbelievable, wealthy life? You'd be outrageous. You'd have lots of fun. Life would be about experiencing the joy of it. It would be about celebration, not diminishment.

Would you please claim and own the capacity to celebrate your life and make it a joyful experience every day, starting today? And would you please claim and own the ability to be out of control?

Chapter Four

DEALING WITH DIFFICULT PEOPLE

ELFs & RATTLESNAKES

An ELF is a person who will undermine you just for the fun of it. What does ELF stand for? Evil Little Fuck (hence my acronym, "ELFs"). An ELF is the person who will say, "Oh, nice dress. I love it every time you wear it!" or "Great dress. It looks good on you, even with all the weight you've gained."

We tend to see other people as either all good or all bad. We want to see the good in them, but not the bad. We think it's unkind to see the bad. Is it? Or is it stupid and insane not to see it? It's stupid and insane. It's also not very conscious. We have to be willing to see the evil in somebody as well as the good.

Have you ever been taken advantage of by someone? Have you ever been used for your money? You have to recognize that there are ELFs and rattlesnakes in the world and some of them are in human bodies.

When a rattlesnake is in a human body, you don't want to take him home for the night. He'll bite your ass one way or another and he'll leave poison in your universe.

Always acknowledge the ELFs and the rattlesnakes in your life. If you don't acknowledge what they are, they can't change. They can't be any different. We know that nobody's all evil, but do rattlesnakes want to be called garter snakes? No. It pisses them off and they want to bite you all the harder. If you acknowledge them and say to yourself, *You're an amazing rattlesnake and you've got great diamonds on your back and boy do you rattle well, and I'm staying eight feet away from you at all times*, then you won't get bitten.

If you can see the evil in someone and acknowledge it, is that a judgment—or is it an observation? If you observe that somebody is willing to do bad things to you, then they can't do those bad things. You only get sucker punched when you're unwilling to look at what somebody's doing that's not kind, not good, or not expansive. Start to see the truth of where people are sitting. Don't buy into the idea that everybody's all good or everybody's all bad.

We've had people come to our classes who are just like snakes. I'll think, *Please God, don't let this one come*, but they keep coming back. They're always a great lesson because I know that eventually they're going to do something mean and nasty. But because I know that, I'm prepared and I can handle it. I don't make the mistake of thinking that just because they're coming to class, they want to get conscious or that they're actually going to get conscious. I know that their choice is to be anti-conscious, and if they're doing anti-consciousness, then they will not be aware of the things they do, and they will choose to dishonor others at every turn.

Who Are the ELFs and Rattlesnakes in Your Life?

Who are the ELFs and rattlesnakes in your life? Will you stop struggling to see the good in them, and stop judging yourself for not being able to do the right thing so they will stop being so mean and nasty?

If you will acknowledge the ELFs and the rattlesnakes around you, not from the viewpoint of judging them, but from awareness, you will create the freedom to steer clear of them — or you will know how to handle them.

We have a friend who is an acupuncturist, and she had a client who was an ELF of magnitude. She asked me what she should do with her, and I said, "Just treat her, but acknowledge that she's an ELF."

My friend called me a few weeks later and said, "I can't believe it! I thought she would be the last person in the world to change, but she came in today and said, 'I've been a terrible person my whole life — I've been mean and nasty to everybody. I've decided I want to be a mother and I can't imagine a child wanting a mother who's mean the way I've been. I'm changing!'"

All you have to do is acknowledge the way someone is. You don't have to try to change them.

PEOPLE WHO DO A SHODDY JOB

Have you known people who don't fulfill their obligations or who do such a shoddy job that you have had to hire somebody else to finish the job they started? Have you wondered how they get away with that? The answer is that if you're not willing to receive everything a person is willing to do, including the good, the bad and the ugly, then you can get screwed.

I had a housekeeper one time. She was somebody I knew, a friend. I came home one day after having worked really hard. I had my kid in my arms as I walked in the door, and I was exhausted. The house was filthy.

> I said, "I thought you cleaned today."
> She said, "I did. You owe me $80."
> I said, "For what? The only thing I can see in this place is that the kitchen counters are clean and the faucets are shiny, but everything else is a mess. The carpet needs vacuuming. The kitchen floor hasn't been cleaned."
> She said, "Well, you owe me."
> I said, "How can I owe you? You haven't done anything. What makes you think you deserve $80?"
> She said, "Because I do."
> I said, "I thought you were my friend. You're going to screw me for $80 because you think you deserve it and you haven't cleaned anything? What kind of friendship is that?"

> She said, "It's just business. Don't take it personally."

Have you ever had anybody do that to you? *It's just business.* Don't you love, *It's just business?* It means they can do anything they want to you and they can be as unethical as they choose and you have to take it, and you're wrong for taking offense. It's just business. It's not personal. Yes, it is personal! When somebody screws you, it's personal.

Have you ever been taken advantage of that way? Are you willing to stand up and be the greatness of you and tell them, "No. I'm not taking it"?

Should You Only See the Good in Others?

How much of you do you have to shut off to not perceive, know, be and receive where somebody truly sits? A lot or a little? A lot. Some people don't want to believe this. They've been taught they should only see the good in others, but if you can't see what is, how can you act appropriately?

You do what is appropriate because you have awareness. You know, *Okay, it's cold enough to put on a jacket.* When you're totally aware, you receive all the information. If you go out into nature expecting it to take care of you, you're not willing to see that it's going to get cold. You're not willing to see that it's going to rain. Do you get drenched? Do you get cold? Yes. In our lives, where we won't perceive what's going to happen, we're naked to the possibilities.

The Idea Is to Become Aware

The idea is to become aware. To allow yourself to receive as you do in nature means you don't cut off your perception and decide, against all the evidence, *Okay, this is a good person to work with.* If you decide someone is honest, and they tell you a lie, are you going to notice? Or are you going to go, *No, she couldn't have lied to me.* She can do that ten times before you finally go, *You know what? She's dishonest!* And then no matter whether she says something truthful or not, you can't hear it. You're *still* not being aware.

You have standards by which you define what you receive from others. If you take away the standards and allow yourself to receive everything from them, then you don't have to have a judgment before you walk in. You can go, *Okay, so who is here in front of me? What's going on? What are they doing?*

If they lie to you, you can say, *Oh, that was a lie. Okay, interesting. I wonder if they've got any other lies they're going to tell.* You can begin to notice what they lie about. And then you realize, *Oh, so if I do this, they're going to lie until they've got all my money, but over here, in this other area of life, they're honest. Okay, cool. I'll buy this part of their deal, but I won't buy that part.*

Are You Willing to Receive All the Information?

If you go into a store where they're selling DVD players and ask for a certain model, and the salesperson tells you, "Oh no, we don't have that model anymore. That one's obsolete," is he telling you the truth? If you're willing to receive all the information the way that you are in nature, you'll know that he's not telling you the truth.

What's really happening is they don't have that model in the store and the salesperson wants to sell you the model they do have. He doesn't want you to get out of the store until you buy something. He won't even say, "Well, I can get you that model." He wants you to buy what they have in stock. If you are willing to receive all the information, then you know what's going on and you can say, *Okay, this isn't really a place I want to do business. They're not going to give me what I'm looking for. They're not interested in serving me. They're only interested in getting my money.*

What do you look for when you go to buy something? Are you looking for a salesperson who's going to take care of you? When you walk in and somebody's really friendly and says, "Hi. It's so nice to see you. Gee, how are you doing?", is she going to take care of you? Is she being real? No. But what about when you walk in and someone says, "Hi. What can I do for you?" If they ask you that question, they might be interested in you.

Who Gave You the Title of God?

If you don't recognize when somebody is doing something unethical, mean-spirited, evil, unkind, divisive or vicious, what happens is you take the responsibility on to yourself. You think, *If I had done that differently, he wouldn't have done what he did. I must have done something wrong. What's wrong with me?*

You aren't willing to recognize that you wouldn't do mean-spirited, unkind things. You might be tempted, but you wouldn't choose that. You take the blame on yourself. Why do you take the blame? Why are you responsible for other people's choices to be mean and unkind? Are you responsible for the entire world? Who gave you the title of God?

I have certainly had that point of view myself. *If I were God, this place would work right.* But when you have that point of view, you always have to look at how, if you had done something differently, the other person would have made a different choice. No. Some people just like to do that kind of stuff. Will you please claim, own and acknowledge that some people just like to be mean?

When You Judge Yourself, Are You Being Aware?

When you blame yourself for what other people do or don't do, whom do you judge? Yourself. And if you judge yourself, are you being aware? Are you able to see that they're choosing to be mean because they like it? No. You assume that you didn't try hard enough, that if you had done it better, they wouldn't have been unkind.

When somebody steals your money, is it because you let them? Is it because you weren't on your toes enough or because you didn't check them out well enough, or is it because they like to steal? Somebody who likes to steal likes to steal. If you come clear on the fact that you are not responsible for the choices other people make, then you can see what they're going to do before they do it.

You just say, *Okay, they're going to choose that. Interesting point of view.* And then when they do it, you say, *You know what? This is enough. I don't want to play this game with you anymore. You can leave now or I will.*

You don't try to make it okay. You don't try to keep a friendship or a business relationship in existence, thinking that if you just got it right or if you did something better or if you changed you, that they would get it and suddenly understand what you're talking about. That's not going to happen.

WHAT DO YOU DO AFTER YOU'VE BEEN DUPED IN A BUSINESS DEAL?

What do you do after you've been duped in a business deal or a relationship? Is it easier to go after somebody to get something back—or to create something new? Instead of looking at the past, at what did or didn't happen, put your attention on how to create a future in which you create more than what you have.

There are people who have stolen parts and pieces of Access and created their own programs based on what they learned from me. Was it theirs? Not an ounce of it. They stole everything from me. They retyped a few things, called things slightly different names and are teaching my material as though the material was theirs. I could sue them because it's my copyrighted material, but I'd rather spend an hour helping somebody who wants to get conscious than fight to stop somebody who's never going to get conscious. Besides, I know the materials they stole aren't going to work for them anyway.

Will Unethical People Eventually Do Themselves In?

Will unethical people eventually do themselves in? No. They don't believe in karma. They are not going to do themselves in. They are going to continue to shaft everybody they can as long as they can. And after they die, they'll come back and do it again because they like to do it. Will you claim, own and acknowledge that some people just like to be mean and nasty? It's one of the things they're good at. It's their forté in life. When somebody's good at something, they'll keep on doing it.

If you are willing to see that someone is an ELF or a rattlesnake, you won't be taken advantage of. You can't be. But because you are kind, caring, loving and all the things you truly are, you often don't see others for what they are. Instead, you judge yourself as wrong. But the reality is you aren't unethical, you aren't vicious, you aren't mean-spirited. Unfortunately, that means you're easygoing, fun-loving, and easily taken advantage of, and everybody sees you as a sucker. But you're only a sucker as long as you're not willing to identify the people who are willing to be mean and vicious.

Can People Take Advantage of You If You Can Perceive What They Are Going to Do?

As long as you're aware, you can't be taken advantage of, because you can say, *No, I'm not going to do that*. You have the choice. As long as you are aware, you won't expect people to do anything differently than what they do.

It's when we expect people to act the way we would act, that we get sucker punched. People will act however they're going to act and you need to be willing to see that. If you're not willing to receive that information, you will be taken advantage of.

You must receive all the information without judgment. Look at what's going on. It's not *Whoa, I need to be careful*. It's *Whoa, I need to be aware*. If you're aware, no one can take advantage of you, but if you're careful, everybody can.

When Dain was looking for a BMW, we went to a lot where they had advertised one for sale. We had called that morning and they said it was still available, but when we got there, the salesman said, "Oh, we sold it already. No big deal. We've got these Porsche Boxsters. A lot of people call for BMWs and I've done this to ten other people. I put them into this car instead."

"I've done this *to* them," he said.
We knew. "Bye! Thank you."
We were out of there.

HOW DO YOU DEAL WITH
ELFs & RATTLESNAKES?

How do you deal with difficult people like ELFs and rattlesnakes? You do it without a vested interest. You don't have a vested interest in the outcome.

When you are asking for something in life, whatever you are asking to receive, you cannot be vested in the outcome. Do you understand what we mean by that? If I think I want to get a million dollars and I've got to get it from you, I'm vested in the outcome. I demand, *Are you going to give me the million dollars? Give me my million dollars!* That's being vested in the outcome.

I've got to get a million dollars translates into I've got to go out and do this — and this — and this. I want a million dollars so I've got to do this $3 million construction process so I've got to eat shit from this person, I've got to eat crow from this person, I've got to let the bankers shaft me at every opportunity, and in the end, it will all work out.

But when you're not vested in the outcome, you can ask, *What are the infinite possibilities of $1 million coming into my life in the next two years or the next year or the next six months?* You allow the information to come to you that will permit you to receive it.

The easiest way to deal with difficult people is to be in allowance. If you recognize the rattlesnake, are you going to get into bed with him? If you recognize the ELF or the rattlesnake, you can say, Interesting point of view. He thinks he can get away with that. If you keep calm, cool and collected and if you're present with what you perceive, you'll know he's going to try and shaft you. You will be aware during the whole conversation and you will not let that happen.

When you say, *Oh, he's really a nice person,* you're dead. When you say, *I'm going to give him back his own medicine,* you've got a fight. When you are in conflict with somebody, the energy gets locked in place. You don't want energy locked in place — you want it to flow. To allow that to happen, you must be in allowance. You're the rock in the stream and the water flows around you. Whatever that difficult person is doing is just an interesting point of view, and when everything is just an interesting point of view, you're the rock in the stream, and the water — or the energy — continues to flow.

SUCK THEM RIGHT OFF THEIR FEET

When I first started teaching, I used to say, *When people are pushing energy at you, you have to be able to pull energy from them so hard that they quit.*

One day I thought, "I hate salesmen, especially when they call at dinnertime. I wonder what would happen if I pulled energy from them." At six o'clock every evening, the phone would start to ring and it was always a salesman and they were always trying to sell me something. I decided to change things. One evening the phone rang and I said, *Okay, this is a salesman. I know it's a salesman.*

> I picked up the phone and said, "Hello," and yes, it was a salesman. He started in his spiel and I started pulling energy from him.
> I said, "That's really cool. I've been looking for these. Can you send me two of them?"
> He said, "Uh, yes sir. Can I have your credit card number?"
> I said, "Sure, no problem" and I was pulling energy from him like mad.
> He took the credit card number and he said, "Are you sure you want this, sir?"
> I said, "Absolutely. This is exactly what I've been looking for."
> I could feel him thinking, "This does not compute, does not compute, does not compute."
> He hung up. Not five minutes later I got a call. "Mr. Douglas? This is so-and-so's supervisor." I was sucking energy like crazy, pulling energy through every pore of my

body and being. He asked, "Did you order this?"
I said, "Yes, sir, I did and I'm really happy it's coming."
He said, "Thank you very much, Mr. Douglas."

People Who Are Doing Sales Need a Barrier

I never got the item, and I never got billed for it. Why? Because people who are doing sales need a barrier. They know you've got a barrier and that if they can knock it down, they've got a sale. But if you don't put up a barrier and you pull energy from them, they think something's wrong—you're crazy, you're a liar or you've got somebody else's credit card. Something's very wrong if you don't have a barrier up and you're not doing resistance and reaction.

I can see salesmen coming to my front door through the window of my house, and when I see them, I start sucking energy from them because I know they are going to try and break down my barriers. The walkway up to the house is flat cement, but because I'm pulling energy, they almost fall down before they get to the door.

> When I open the door, I say, "Hi, how are you doing?" and I pull energy.
> They say, "Hi, I'm selling this and it's no good and you really don't want it."
> I keep pulling energy, and they say, "Never mind. Bye."

They have no idea why they said those things to me.

A car salesman will say, "I have this really great truck and it's really drivable." When you pull energy, he'll say, "And the transmission is about to go out on it and it's really not worth this kind of money. I can't believe I said that!" They do it all the time. You've just got to suck energy like crazy when they're pushing energy at you.

If you pull massively from somebody who's pushing energy at you, they'll tell you all the reasons why you shouldn't buy their product. It also works with religious people who come to your door. If you allow them to come in, and you just pull energy from them like crazy, they'll go away.

Religious people would come to my house and I'd know who they were and I'd open the door and I'd pull energy like crazy and I'd say, "Hi, how are you?"

> And they'd go, "Hi, we're here on behalf of God," or whatever.
> I'd say, "Cool. I'd be glad to listen to everything you've got to say. Would you mind if I channel for you?"

Speed of light, they were out of there and my house was put on the list of houses to avoid. They never came back again.

How Do You Pull Energy?

How do you pull energy? You just ask the energy to pull. Someone recently told me how it worked with a policeman. She got pulled over for speeding and she sucked energy. Instead of giving her a ticket, the policeman said, "Don't do it again." You can use this in all kinds of places. As long as you suck energy from somebody, they can't do their aggressive behavior. Aggression stops when you pull energy.

One of the things you can do to practice this is go into a coffee shop, some place where there are lots of people. Just stand to the side of the door and pull energy from every person in the place until they all turn around and look at you.

You just ask the energy to pull. *Okay, I'm going to pull energy from everybody in this place until they all turn around and look at me.*

People will turn and look at you, and you'll go, *Cool!* That's all it takes. There's no work. It doesn't take effort. It's easy.

HOW DO YOU GET MONEY THAT IS OWED TO YOU?

Sometimes people ask me, "How do I get money that is owed to me?" If somebody owes you money, the thing to do is to pull energy from them through every pore of your body and being until you feel your heart open up. When that occurs, you've connected with them. Then you let a little trickle go back to them. Keep doing this every day, twenty-four hours a day. They won't be able to get you off their mind until they pay you back.

Do this without being vested in the outcome. Decide that you're going to maintain this connection to them and you're going to keep letting the flow of energy come towards you until the money you're owed comes with the flow.

How Does It Work?

When somebody owes you money, they put up a barrier. If you pull energy from them and let a little trickle go back, they can't stop thinking about you. The more they think about you, the more guilty they feel. The more guilty they feel, the more likely they are to pay you. It works!

Are you trying to collect money from someone who has died? Do the same thing. He'll come to you in another body and give you some kind of money and you'll wonder, *Why is this guy giving me this money?* He went out and got a new body, and he's come back. You're an unlimited being, right? Do you think it's only one lifetime that counts?

Have you ever had the experience of somebody coming in and spending a lot of money on you or buying something from you or giving you a job or big sum of money and you had no idea why they were doing it? They had no real connection to you and they came and gave you a big sum of money you didn't really earn? They dropped off the money and went out of your life? If that's happened to you it's because that person owed you from another lifetime.

Chapter Five

GIFTING AND RECEIVING

LEARNING TO RECEIVE IS THE GREATEST THING YOU CAN DO

We've worked with lots of people regarding their money issues. We've worked

with people who had $10 in their pocket and people who had $10 million. The interesting thing is they all have the same issue—and it has nothing to do with money at all. It has to do with what they are willing to receive.

Learning to receive is the greatest thing you can do. The limitation of money, the limitation of sex, the limitation of relationship, the limitation of anything at all in your life, is based on what you are unwilling to receive. What you are unwilling to receive creates the limitation of what you can have.

JUDGMENT LIMITS YOUR CAPACITY TO RECEIVE

Whenever you go into judgment about anything, whether it is a positive judgment or a negative judgment—or any degree of judgment—you cut off your capacity to receive beyond that judgment. Every judgment you make stops you from receiving anything that doesn't match it, so even a positive judgment like, *This person is perfect,* keeps you from seeing when they're not perfect. If you decide you have married the perfect woman, are you able to see when she's not perfect? Can you see when she's cheating on you? No. You are not able to receive the full reality of that person.

Whatever we are unable to receive is based on our judgments. Do you need to live in judgment? No. In fact, you need to live without judgment. If you live from a place of no judgment, you can receive the entirety of the world. You can have everything you've always wanted. When you have no judgment, there isn't anything you can't receive.

I worked with a man who had a men's clothing store in a gay section of town. He was having trouble with his business and he asked me to help him sort out what the problem was. We examined everything, and it all looked pretty good, and I was thinking, What's keeping him from being successful?

> I said, "So, tell me about your customers."
> He said, "Oh, they're pretty nice except for those guys."
> I said, "Those guys? Who are those guys?"
> He said, "Oh, you know, the swishy queens that come in. I hate it when they come in and hit on me."
> I said, "Your shop is in the gay area of town, correct?"
> He said, "Yes."

I said, "You know what? You have made a mistake here because you will not receive your customers' energy. They're not going to give you any money if you're not willing to have their energy.

He said, "What do you mean?"

I said, "You have to be willing to receive their energy if you would have their money. You have to learn to banter and flirt with them."

He said, "I could never do that! I don't want to have sex with a man!"

I said, "I didn't say you had to have sex with them. I said you had to flirt with them. You'll flirt with a woman, won't you?"

He said, "When my wife's not around."

I said, "Then just flirt with a man. It doesn't mean you have to copulate with him. It just means you are willing to receive the energy he's giving you and then you can have his money."

So he learned to enjoy his customers and to banter and flirt with them. He learned to have a good time with them and he started making lots of money. He had a judgment about receiving the energy of his customers, which created a limitation on what he could receive financially. The same is true for you. What you are unwilling to receive energetically becomes the limitation of what you can create money from.

WHAT ARE YOU ABSOLUTELY UNWILLING TO RECEIVE?

We're going to ask you a question and we'd like you to write down the first thing that pops into your head—or say it out loud, especially if it makes absolutely no sense to you. The purpose of this question is to unlock what you're unwilling to receive. Whatever we're unwilling to receive creates a limitation of what we can create in our lives. It limits what we can have.

Here is the question: What are you absolutely unwilling to receive, that if you were willing, would manifest as total abundance?

We asked this question of a group of people. These are some of the answers they came up with. Do any of them apply to you?

People disliking me	*Judgments*	*Health*
Love	*Sex*	*Self*
Intimacy		

What are you absolutely unwilling to receive, that if you were willing, would manifest as total abundance? What's on your list? Are your answers anything like these?

Responsibility	*The greatness of me*
Success	*Something I have to slave for*
Being weird and different	*Feeling good about having fun in my life*

What are you absolutely unwilling to receive, that if you were willing, would manifest as total abundance? What did you come up with this time? Do your answers contain any of these items?

Easy money	*Being overwhelmed*	*Caring*
Being wrong	*The ability to create*	*Help*
Being slapped in the face	*Being joyful*	*Taking risks*

Pretty interesting, isn't it? The things you're unwilling to receive limit what you can have in life. Because you aren't willing to receive these things, you cannot have abundance. Everybody has pretty much the same issues. Your unwillingness to receive whatever came up for you, limits the amount of money you can have. It limits what you can have in every respect. It's what we are unwilling to receive that makes the problem. What if you were willing to receive anything and everything?

What energy have you decided you cannot receive? What judgment do you have that stops you from receiving unlimitedly? As you read these questions, you may have something pop into your head. It will be an answer from—guess where—your insane mind, because that's what creates all your limitations. Your logical mind takes these insane limitations and justifies them. It provides the decisions and judgments that keep the limitation in existence.

The great thing about this is: the response from your insane mind that pops into your head is not only a statement of your limitation, it's also the answer that will set you free. Your logical mind only provides justifications for the insane point of view you already have.

So, what energy are you unwilling to receive?

I Don't Screw Around with Married Women

Years ago when I was in my thirties, I trained horses. At the time, I was planning to go to Europe for six months and I met a lady who lived in Montecito, which is a ritzy area of Santa Barbara. She had some horses she wanted me to ride, so I went and rode her horses. She thought I was really cute and was checking me out and hitting on me. My reaction to this was a judgment: *I don't screw around with married women.* She had an attorney for a husband and I thought the last thing I wanted to do is get myself involved in that kind of thing. I could be in real trouble.

So, I went away to Europe, and I was gone six months. When I came back, she started calling me, and based on my earlier judgment, I just put her off, and put her off and didn't have anything to do with her.

Two months later I found out that she married a guy who looked so much like me he could have been my brother. I had assumed she was married—but the reality was she had divorced her husband while I was in Europe. Nobody had told me.

Six months after her marriage she died of a cerebral hemorrhage and she left her new husband $67 million dollars. Do you think my judgments had any effect on my life? What judgments of yours might be having an equally detrimental effect on your life?

OUT OF CONTROL vs. UN-CONTROL

We tend to control ourselves with the limitations we create. We create controls around ourselves about what we will receive, what we won't receive, what is possible, what is not possible, what we think it's got to look like, and what we want it to look like. We think this puts us in control. But you don't want to be in control—you want to be out of control. You have to get to the point where you're willing to be totally out of control.

I'm not talking about being out of control in the sense of being drunk and disorderly, nor am I talking about speeding at 8,000 m.p.h. down the freeway. I'm not talking about getting naked in public or that sort of thing. That's un-control. What you want to be is out of control. The problem in your life is that you are not out of control.

We tend to spend a lot of our time sitting in judgment, trying to figure out how to control ourselves so we can get along in the world. When we are out of control, we are willing to exist outside of the normal box and the normal points of reference. Being out of control is not being uncontrolled and it's not being drunk and disorderly. It's about not letting the controls of other people's points of view, other people's realities, judgments and decisions be the controlling factor in our lives. Being out of control is taking away those things, where you've giving away parts of your life to others and have made them more powerful than you. To be out of control is to no longer be the effect, but to be the source.

You want to be out of control because you've defined your life. You have the box of your life defined and confined. You have created the coffin you call your life. You think you're alive but you're living within a coffin. If you would break down those confines, you could start to create from a sense of out of control.

Once you are willing to be out of control, you're willing to be out of the coffin you've created your life as. You don't look to past experience as the source of what you're going to create in the future. You'll start to live in the moment. Instead of trying to come up with answers based on your limited points of view, you empower the universe to give you the answer.

GIVE-AND-TAKE vs. GIFTING AND RECEIVING

This world is pretty much based on the practice of give-and-take. It's a point of view that says, I give you this; you give me that. It's an exchange modality we're all stuck in. If I give you oral sex, then you feel obligated to give me oral sex. It's an exchange. I do this, now you must do that.

With gifting, on the other hand, there is no separate exchange that occurs. You give without expectation of return, and as a result you simultaneously receive without limit. The gifting is the receiving, and the receiving is the gifting, all at the same time. With gifting and receiving, you have the elements that allow you to truly have a sense of communion with all things. When you go out in nature, for example, does it gift to you? Does it expect anything in return?

Nature gifts everything it has at all times and it simultaneously receives from everything. The fruit trees create the fruit and gift to you totally. Do they hold any of it back?

When you have a flowerbed full of beautiful flowers, they gift to you their fragrance and their beauty and they ask nothing in return. What they receive from you is the energy you give them and the gratitude you have for their beauty.

Rather than gifting and receiving, most of us live in the world of give-and-take. We say, "I'm going to give you this, but I expect something in return." We give a gift with the idea we're going to get something back. How many times, when you are given something, do you know the giver expects you to do, give, contribute or function in some way for them? Most of the time? That's right. *If I give you this, then you must give me that.* It's give-and-take.

When you live in the give-and-take world, you eliminate gifting. This is a terrible mistake, because when you gift to somebody, truly gift to them, you simultaneously receive abundantly, beyond anything you can imagine. If you truly gift without expectation, then you receive abundantly in all respects. But for the most part, on this planet, we give only when we are obligated to do so. What we have at work is the give-and-take reality of exchange, not abundance.

What would it be like in your world if you had the generosity of spirit that allowed you to give without ever expecting anything in return? Wouldn't that be wonderful? Why don't you allow that to come into your life? Maybe it's because you don't expect people to receive what you give them—and they don't.

People Who Cannot Receive

People who cannot receive what you give return your gift to you with a couple of daggers attached. They have to show you how much they didn't like it because they were unable to receive it in the first place.

A woman told me about her father. She tried to tell him how much she cared about him and he answered, "Yes-yes, darling, okay." He couldn't receive it. When you try to give to somebody who can't receive what you're saying or what you're gifting, they will always negate it. Why is that? They don't believe that it's okay to receive.

People Who Give Too Much

Some people give and give and give, thinking others will be happy with them for giving so much. Is this gifting? No, because it's expecting a return. Does it work? Does the other person get happy with them? No. Usually they say, *Oh, I'll take more of that — and more of that — and what else do you have? I'll take that, too.*

Have you ever done the give-too-much routine? Do you give your children too much? Are they grateful for what you give them? With my kids, it seems the more I give them, the more they take. Children, as my friend Mary says, will take your last breath and never say thank you. They expect you to give to them all the time, and they'll always take from you. They don't see that there needs to be an honoring of the gift. They don't consider what you give them to be a gift; they think whatever you give is due them.

Whenever you're giving to somebody who feels *entitled* to receive, or who thinks you *should* give because you've got the money or because you can — it's not very clean. There will be no real joy in your giving, or in the receipt of it. If you have a friend who doesn't have enough, you might try to give to him in order to help him, and then pretty soon you might find you are giving to him all the time, and there's no end to it. This is what happens when you're on the give-and-take program. Is it possible, in doing all this giving, that you believe you really shouldn't receive? Is it possible that you feel you must always give, but never receive?

Some people give in order to make others feel less-than. We know a woman who was giving hugely expensive gifts to people all the time. One of her friends who was troubled by this said to me, "I can't give her anything in return because I can't equal the amount of money she has spent on me." We talked about this for a while and she realized her friend's giving was a way of pushing other people away, so that even as they were receiving more, they would feel less-than.

Give-and-take and gifting and receiving occur in relationships of every kind. If you're in a relationship where you think you have to give 150 percent, you usually end up with someone who is willing to take 150 percent. You do not get someone who gives as much as you do. But when you are truly gifting and receiving in relationship, the person gifts to you and receives simultaneously as a result. You gift to them, and you receive simultaneously.

Do You Live in the Ledger and Balance Sheet World of Give-and-Take?

Often when people have been kept from having things, they develop a point of view which says, *This is mine and I know how much I have and you'd better not try to take one of my nuts, damn it.* They live in the ledger and balance sheet world of give-and-take. Do you know people who have to keep the accounts balanced? They say things like, "The bill is $37.50. If we divide it, that's $18.75 each. Okay, you owe me $18.75." "This is my food. Don't eat my avocados!" The end result of this kind of thinking is that they have no abundance. You cannot live in the ledger and balance sheet world and believe in the abundance of your life. What would happen if you took a completely different point of view: *You want it? Take it!*

When you get rid of the idea, I've got to get my share, you can experience the abundance of the universe. If you're totally abundant, do you care if your roommate eats the avocado you thought was yours? If you are an unlimited being with unlimited resources, with unlimited possibility, how can you ever be taken from? Really. Can you ever truly over-gift?

The Universe Is Endlessly Abundant

One of the ways I changed my own point of view about gifting and receiving was to practice giving without expectation. A friend and I went to a restaurant one time. I ordered a cup of coffee and a donut and my friend ordered a cup of tea. Our waitress was about forty-five years old. First she brought my friend a spoon, then she went back and got me a spoon. Then she brought me the cup of coffee. Then she went back and got the tea, then the cream, and then the donut.

I asked, "Are you having a tough day?"
She got teary-eyed and said, "I've never worked before. This is the first job I've ever had. I don't know how to do this. I'm overwhelmed."
I said, "Don't worry, it'll get better. You'll get used to it."
She said, "Thank you. That's very kind."
She brought us the bill and it was $5.12. I left her $10.12.
As we were walking out the door, she came running after us, "Sir, sir, you gave me too much money!"
I said, "No I didn't. That's a tip. It's to let you know you're doing okay." You could see the beams in her universe.

Another time, I was walking in New York on my way to lunch and there was a young guy sitting on the street with a big open cut on his leg and a tin can in front of him. No one was putting any money into it. On my way back from lunch, without looking at him, I stuck a $20 bill in the can, and he went, "Thank you, sir. Oh my God! Bless you! Bless you! Thank you!" I could feel the energy radiating out of him because someone had seen, acknowledged and gifted to him without any expectation. Not a quarter, not a nickel—not: *Okay, you're a little bum*—but enough that he could actually afford a good meal.

If you do those sorts of things, you break down the idea that there's no abundance in the world. You have to do it. You have to make it happen.

When I was moving out of my house after my divorce, I had a bunch of antiques I was going to sell, but instead of doing that, I gave them to my friend, the antique dealer, who had more money than I did. I gave all my antiques to him, and it confused the hell out of him. He couldn't understand why I would gift to him because he had more than I did. His point of view was you have to give to someone who has less than you. That's a concept you have to get over.

When people who have lots of money go out with people who have less, those with less money usually expect those with more to pay. When I go out to dinner with people who have lots of money, I always make it a point to pay. They don't know what to do with that. I'm not less than they are anymore. You can play with this, too. Pick up the check once in a while. See what happens.

The purpose of life is to have fun, and maybe the purpose of money is to bust people's paradigms. What you're really doing, though, is living from the idea that the universe is endlessly abundant, and when you function from that, everything in life gets better.

HUMAN OR HUMANOID: WHICH ARE YOU?

One of the more unexpected things we've discovered in our work with Access is the awareness that there appear to be two species of beings on planet Earth, humans and humanoids.

Humans live in judgment of everybody else and think that life is just the way it is, and nothing is ever right, they don't even bother to think about another possibility.

Humanoids look for ways to make things better. If you invent things, if you search out things, if you are always looking for a better, bigger way of creating something, you are a humanoid, not a human. Humanoids are the people who create change. They create the inventions, the music and the poetry. They create all the changes that come out of a lack of satisfaction with the status quo.

"Well, If You'd Just Get a TV . . ."

For humanoids, it is a great relief to know that we are always judged and we never fit in. We try so hard, but we can't make ourselves fit into the human mold. Most of us desperately seek to understand and fit into the human reality of money — and everything else. People tell us, "Well, if you'd just get a TV, a new car and a regular job, you'd be fine."

The idea of bringing up the differences between humans and humanoids is not about sitting in judgment of humans. It's about becoming aware of how we humanoids judge ourselves.

Humanoids Judge Themselves

One of the most important things to know about humanoids is that they sit in judgment of themselves. Humanoids think there's something wrong with themselves because they're not like everyone else around them. They ask themselves, "What's wrong with me that I can't get it right? Why can't I be like this other person? Why can't I be satisfied with less? What's wrong with me?" They go into serious amounts of judgments of themselves. They wonder why they can't get what everyone else gets and do what everybody else does.

When somebody lies to a humanoid, or does something wrong to them, humanoids twist it around and look for what they've done wrong. They make themselves wrong and the other person right. A humanoid friend of mine had been in a business relationship with a partner for a long time and one day he was talking about how his business never seemed to make any money.

> I said, "There's something wrong here. You'd better have a look at the books. I think your partner's cheating you."
> He said, "Oh, he would never cheat me."
> I asked him, "Can you look into this?"

He decided to have a closer look at the books, and when his business partner found out what he was doing, the partner got really angry and made a lot of accusations against him. My friend's response was to judge himself hideously for being so disloyal as to question his partner.

A month later my friend found out his partner was cheating him.

My humanoid friend's response to the discovery that his partner was cheating him was to heap huge amounts of judgment on himself, whereas his human partner's response was, "This is all your fault. If you weren't such a crappy partner, none of this would have happened."

This Is All There Is

Humans do not have the slightest idea that they're infinite beings with infinite possibilities. They don't believe in reincarnation. They think this is all there is. They say things like, "You live, you die and you become worm food."

> I talked to my stepdad, who was very definitely human, after he had a heart attack. I said, "Dad, what was it like for you having that heart attack?" Nobody had asked him that question.
> He said, "Well, I remember having the heart attack and standing outside my body looking at it . . ." He trailed off, and then started over again.
> "Well, I had the heart attack and then I saw them putting the electrodes on my chest . . ." Again, he stopped mid-sentence, waited a moment, and then started over again.
> "Well," he finally, said, "I had the heart attack and then they put the electrodes on my chest and they zapped me."

He could not have a reality in which he was out of his body watching these things occur. It was a great example of what happens to people when they can't have what doesn't fit their judgment of reality. His reality was that you are in a body and that's all there is. A human can never have anything that doesn't match the viewpoint, This is all there is. Humans do not believe in other possibilities. They do not believe in miracles or magic. The doctors and the lawyers and the Indian chiefs create everything. Humans create nothing.

Forty-seven percent of the population is humanoid and they are the creators of everything that changes in this planet Earth reality. Fifty-two percent is human. (And the final one percent? Some day we'll tell you about them!) Humans hold onto things the way they are and never want anything to change. Have you ever been to somebody's house where they haven't changed the furniture in thirty years? Human.

Humans will live in the same neighborhood until it goes downhill, and rather than moving, they will put bars over their windows to keep the jailbirds out of their house. And who's looking out of the bars? Excuse me, you've just made yourself into a jailbird! Humans are the contractors who tear out all of the plants and trees so they can remodel a house. They kill everything in order to create. "That's just the way it is," they say. "We're going to kill everything, and it will be fine."

Humans sit in judgment of others, because everything in their life is about judgment, decisions, force and effort. It's the only place they create from. Think of somebody you know who's human. Feel the consciousness of him or her. Now feel the consciousness of a rock. Which one is lighter? The rock? Okay. There's more consciousness in the rock, so we hang out with humans for what reason? We all have human friends and family, but they sit in judgment of us and tell us how wrong we are for everything we do. Humans' judgments of us are compounded by the fact that we as humanoids tend to judge ourselves.

Acknowledge That You Are a Humanoid

What happens if you don't claim the totality of your humanoid capacity? If you don't understand and acknowledge that you are humanoid, you try to create from a human point of view. You believe in—and create—a limited possibility for yourself. A human will say, "Show me the steps," and will diligently do each step one at a time, but you, as a humanoid, have the ability to zoom from A to Z, just like that. You can go bam-bam and have anything you desire, but most of us do not claim that possibility for ourselves. We try to settle ourselves into a human existence.

This is a mistake, because humans are content with the status quo and don't want anything to change—and humanoids want to expand and be abundant and creative. If you are interested in expansion, and in having a life that is abundant, comfortable and creative, stop trying to stuff yourself into a human mold. Acknowledge that you're a humanoid — and claim your capacity to join the ranks of the rich and famous.

HUMANOIDS, WORK AND MONEY

Humanoids Don't Work for Money

One of the very interesting differences between humans and humanoids is that humanoids don't work for money. When a humanoid creates something or performs a service and someone else truly receives it, they feel complete. For them, that's the exchange. They say, "Wow. That's cool!", and they're done. Their gift has been accepted. That's the end of the exchange. Their energy is complete on it.

Money has nothing to do with a humanoid's creative capacity or what motivates them. The money is a by-product. It's a secondary result. It's like shit. Most humanoids would prefer not to deal with money and not to put attention on it, because it has nothing to do with their creative capacity. For them, the work or the creation was the fun part. After they create something, they look around and ask, "What else can I create?" Creation moves the energy for them. All the energy in a humanoid universe goes into creation.

If you're a humanoid, and we think you are, it's important to be aware of this, because unless you are willing to receive the by-product of your work or service, you're not going to get the money. You're actually going to push it away. You'll stop the money from coming in. You're going to refuse to collect it even though it's due to you. You won't ask for it.

When it's time to ask for money, humanoids go, *Ahmm...would you like to pay me now or later?* It's hard for them to collect money for their work because really, all they want is for their gift to be received.

Humans, on the other hand, are clear: they work for money. A human contractor or land developer will go into a place and destroy all the trees and everything that lives on the land and build something new made out of concrete because of the money he's going to get for it. He can do it for the money.

Humanoids get confused because they can't do things for money, yet the point of view they grew up with is, *You only do things for money, and if you don't get paid for it, it's not worth doing.* We try to fit into the human reality of money, and this causes us great difficulty. We have to understand that as humanoids we have a different view, and we also have to be willing to receive the by-product of our endeavors. We have to be able to ask for — and receive — money.

Chapter Six

CELEBRATE YOUR ABUNDANCE

ARE YOU SHARING THE POVERTY OF THE UNIVERSE INSTEAD OF ITS ABUNDANCE?

Some people feel they have received more than their fair share in life and they live in judgment of themselves because they have more than others. They were taught that they had to share everything and nobody's supposed to have more than anyone else. In their family, the pie was cut in equal pieces, except for Dad. He usually got a bigger piece because he was the breadwinner.

Is it possible that you have bought a similar story? Are you living the equal share reality? Are you sharing the poverty of the universe instead of its abundance? Let me ask you: What's wrong with sharing the abundance of the universe instead of the poverty? Wouldn't you like to give up poverty as the truth of you? Wouldn't you rather share in the vast abundance of the universe?

You're a Totally Abundant Person

Have you had lifetimes in which you were filthy rich? Yes, you have. Do you keep wondering, *Where the hell's the money this lifetime? It was supposed to show up by now, damn it.*

Have you had lifetimes in which you were totally broke? You bet. How many lifetimes did you only just survive? And are you continuing to merely survive? Are you willing to give up merely surviving as a point of view?

Get the feeling you've had of, *Oh my God, I'm barely surviving.* Make it infinite, bigger than the universe. What happens to it? Does it get more substantial or does it go away? It goes away, which means it's a lie. You as an infinite being cannot merely survive. You're totally abundant.

This universe, even on planet Earth, is an incredibly abundant place. The only reason there is a bare patch anywhere is because humans have been stupid enough to take everything away from it. Nature will fill every square inch with something. When you go to the desert, is it empty? No. Even in the desert, there is life everywhere. There are plants, bugs and critters of all kinds. Every square inch is covered with something.

How can you live as not abundant? You do it by buying into the idea that there's scarcity. You adopt the point of view that there is no abundance because you aren't able to figure out where it's going to come from. You don't see that abundance is actually all around you.

We think, *Oh, in the future I'll have money,* or *In the past I used to have money,* but we don't see that we are totally abundant now.

Are You Embracing the Idea That Money Can Be Here Right Now?

Close your eyes right now and see money coming at you. Is it coming from the back or the front, from the right or the left, or from the up or the down? If you see money coming from in front of you, the idea is that you're going to have it in the future. But when does the future arrive? Never. You're always looking for money out in front of you. You are like the donkey with the carrot in front of his face. You're always going for a future event.

If you see money coming at you from the right, then the point of view is you've got to work hard for it. If it's coming from the left, the point of view is that it will come as a handout. Somebody's going to give you a handout to get you rich.

Did you see it coming from behind you? That means you used to have it but you ain't gonna have it anymore.

If you saw it coming from the top, that means you think God's going to give it to you because nobody else will.

Did you see it coming from the ground? Then you'd better become a farmer, because that's where you think it's going to come from. It's going to grow underneath your feet. Or you could go out and become an opal miner and find it that way.

What Would It Be Like If You Let Money Come to You from All Directions?

What would it be like if you let money come to you all the time, and from all directions? Get that feeling right now. Now, make that infinite, bigger than the universe. Does it get more substantial or less? Keep that feeling and you'll have money tomorrow.

The idea of this visualization is to get clear about where you think money comes from. If you have the idea that it's going to come from the future, you're not embracing the idea that money can be here right now. If you look at it as tomorrow, tomorrow, tomorrow, then today's bills get paid when? Tomorrow or yesterday, or they don't get paid at all. This keeps you in a cycle of hustling to take care of things instead of being present with what's available to you.

If you were truly conscious, if you were in communion with all things, if you were being the humanoid you truly are, and if you were functioning from the aesthetics of time, space, dimensions and realities in which no judgment can exist, money could simply be part of your life rather than the end-all.

Guess What Having Money Is All About?

Most people make money the goal or they make it a need. They say things like, *If I only had____* or *If I just had____* or *Money will make me ____*. None of those are real. Those are ideas we have substituted for actually allowing ourselves to have everything that is possible in our lives. When you do that, you're making money into something that's terribly significant rather than seeing it like a flower that grows in your garden. If you spend as much time nurturing money, feeding it, fertilizing it, watering it, and taking care of it the way you do your flowers, do you think it might grow in your life? I'm not suggesting that you plant money in the ground, but I do know it will work if you think of it in those terms. Do you have to be able to receive money? Absolutely. You have to be open to receiving. Guess what having money is all about? The ability to receive.

What About Self-Reliance?

Sometimes people ask me: *What about self-reliance?* I ask them back: *Why would you want to be self-reliant? Wouldn't you rather be able to receive everything?* All things are possible when you're willing to receive.

Most of us have made decisions like *I have to rely on myself*, which means we're all alone out there. When you have the idea,

I'm self-reliant, I'm all alone, I'm doing it on my own, I'm going to make it on my own, how much help are you willing to receive? None. How much help do you get? None. You're so busy proving you have to do it on your own, that you won't let others assist you in creating money. You're doing, *I will prove I don't need anybody. I don't care what you say. I don't need you. Go away.*

The truth, of course, is that money likes to serve you. It thinks its job is to be your slave. You didn't know that, did you? Money thinks it's supposed to be of service. Someone who is of service is your slave or your servant. Would you like to give up serving money and let money serve you from now on?

WHAT IF YOU CELEBRATED YOUR LIFE EVERY DAY?

If you don't celebrate your life, if you don't make your life a celebration, if you create your life so it's about the obligation, the work, the trauma, the drama, the upset, and the intrigue, what will show up in your life? More of the same. But if you begin to create your life as a celebration, different possibilities will show up.

When my ex-wife and I got divorced, I moved out of our house, and I took very little with me. I left with one set of good china out of five, one set of sterling silver flatware out of five, one frying pan, one spatula, one spoon and the carving set that had belonged to my father. I took a set of old dishes, the ones that my ex-wife didn't like that had chips in all of them, a couple of funky old glasses that nobody wanted and a couple of coffee mugs that were uglier than sin. That was the sum total of my kitchenware. Those were the things I moved into my new place.

I put the good china away for the celebrations and the dinner parties I would give some day. I'm sure I was going to do service for sixteen on my tiny round table, right? And I put all the ugly, old stuff I had brought into my kitchen cupboard.

Then one day I looked at it and I said, "Wait a minute. I'm saving this stuff for a celebration, and I am living like a pauper. Whose life am I living, anyway? Mine? I want my life to be a celebration."

I got out all the good china, and I said, "If I break a cereal bowl in the morning when I eat my breakfast, it will cost me $38 to replace it. But who cares? My plates, if I break them, cost $16 apiece. So what? I'll use the Georgian sterling silver flatware. My spoons cost $360 apiece. I'm worth it."

I went out and I bought crystal glasses to drink out of. No more of those thick, old glasses that wouldn't break even if you threw them on the floor. I wanted something that when I knocked it over by accident went, CRASH!

Life needs to be a celebration. If you aren't celebrating your life, you're not living. Life should be an orgasmic experience every day. You shouldn't live with what you've got to put up with, what you've got to do, and what's left over. Are you going to spend your life as a package of leftovers or are you going to create yourself as a celebration?

I have champagne—not cheap-shit champagne—but good champagne, at least five bottles in my refrigerator at all times. Sometimes I have champagne and pie for dinner just because I can.

If you make your life a celebration, if you look for the joy of life instead of the doldrums, you'll create a whole different reality. Isn't that what you really would like to have?

Today Ought to Be the Best Day of Your Life

When I went to my brother-in-law's fortieth birthday party, all the men were in the living room talking about how the best time of their lives were when they were eighteen and in high school. They had cool cars and were jocks. All the women were in the kitchen talking about how the best time in their lives were when their babies were born. When it was my turn to talk they asked me, "When was the best time of your life?"

I said, "Today, and if it isn't, I'm blowing my f------ brains out." I was not very popular after that. Today ought to be the best day of your life. If today isn't the best day of your life, why the hell are you alive?

Just for Today, My Life Will Be a Celebration

Remind yourself every day to make your life a celebration. Look for the joy of life. Every morning say, *Just for today, my life will be a celebration*, and watch for the new possibilities that will show up.

ASK FOR THE GREATNESS OF YOUR LIFE

Ask and ye shall receive is one of the truths in the Bible.

So what are you going to ask for? The greatness of you? If you ask for the greatness of you to show up, then all kinds of other things will come along with it. Ask for the greatness of your life. Ask for the joy and the celebration of your life. Don't just ask for money because money doesn't have anything to do with the greatness of your life. You do.

If you ask for the greatness of your life, if you ask for the greatness of who you are, and if you ask for your life to be a celebration, then you're going to have infinite possibilities. If you only ask for money, nothing's going to show up because money is not the energy. Money is only the vehicle you use to get there. Ask for the greatness of you.

If you have the courage to ask, you can receive.

WHEN ALL IS SAID AND DONE,
WHAT DO YOU REALLY HAVE?

Recently some Gulf Coast hurricane survivors were being interviewed on television. The interviewer asked a guy whose home had been destroyed, "How do you feel about the hurricane?" and the man said, "Well, you know, I moved down here to the Gulf Coast and I brought all my worldly possessions, all my family photos, everything I thought was valuable to me, and now all I have is a slab. Everything I owned blew away in the wind. But you know what? I still have me."

The same thing happened after a big earthquake in California. An interviewer on television asked a guy, "How do you feel about the earthquake?" and the man said, "My wife and I were in the bedroom on the third floor of our condo. I was sound asleep. I had no clothes on. All of a sudden there was a big shake and suddenly I was on the ground. I didn't know where anything was, and there next to me were a pair of shorts, so I put them on. My wife found her robe lying next to her. The only other thing we managed to find was a picture of my wife when we got married. We have no idea where our clothes are. We have no idea where anything is. We can't find a thing. But you know what? We still have each other."

When all is said and done, what do you really have?

You.

You're the starting point for your life. You're the starting point for the creation of your money, your wealth, your power and everything else. Regardless of what the disaster is, regardless of what goes away or is lost, you will always have you. You're the starting point for everything that happens in your life.

YOU CAN CHANGE THE WAY MONEY FLOWS INTO YOUR LIFE

• Put away ten percent of everything you take in. Tithe to the Church of You.

• Carry lots of money in your pocket—but don't spend it.

• Ask yourself the Perceive, Know, Be and Receive question for several days—or for several weeks—until you start to see a change. It's a great technique for becoming aware of what's limiting you. *Perceive, know, be and receive what I refuse, dare not, must never and must also perceive, know, be and receive that will allow me total clarity and ease with _____. Or use a simplified version: What must I perceive, know, be and receive that would allow me to ____?*

• Do not judge yourself. Understand that you are humanoid. That gives you an unfair advantage over the rest of the world. Take it! Does your life reflect that? Do you have lots of money? You will.

• When you start judging yourself, ask, *Is this mine?* Ninety-eight percent of your thoughts, feelings and emotions do not belong to you. You are way more psychic than you give yourself credit for. When you start to ask yourself, *Is this mine?*, you'll become very clear about the fact that you have no thoughts. You're essentially an airhead.

• Live your life in ten-second increments. If you do not live in ten-second increments, you are not living in choice. If you are constantly creating in ten-second increments, you cannot make a mistake, because for ten seconds you can make a stupid and insane choice and ten seconds later you can change it.

• Use energy flows. If you're trying to get connected to somebody or if you would like them to pay you the money they owe, pull energy from them through every pore of your body and your being and let a little trickle go back to them so they can't get you off their mind. They'll have no peace. It will drive them crazy until they pay you.

• Start paying attention to what you're creating. Does it make you happy? If things keep showing up a certain way, there's something about them that you love. If life keeps showing up with no money, no friends and no-something-else, it's because there's something about that which you love to create. Once you acknowledge, *Okay, I must love it, I don't know why, but okay, I love it*, things can begin to change.

• Live in the question. A question empowers. An answer disempowers. If what you are getting in life is not what you'd like to have, notice what are you truly asking for and what you're getting. How do you change that? Ask a different question. When you ask a question the universe will do everything it can to give you the answer. It's not: Oh my God, my life sucks. It's: *What are the infinite possibilities of something different showing up in my life?*

• When money shows up in your life ask, *How does it get any better than this?* When a bill shows up in your life ask, *How does it get any better than this?* (Maybe you'll find out it was a mistake.) Keep asking, *How does it get any better than this?*, whether it's good or bad and the universe will do whatever it can to make it better.

• Say: *All of life comes to me with ease and joy and glory.* It's our mantra in Access: All of life comes to me with ease and joy and glory. It's not an affirmation because it's not about having only the positive. It includes the good, the bad and the ugly. We'll take it all with ease and joy and glory. None of it has to be painful, suffering and gory, even though that's the way most of us live our lives. You can have fun instead. What if the purpose of life was merely to have fun? All of life comes to me with ease and joy and glory. Say it ten times in the morning and ten times in the evening and it will change your life. Put it on your bathroom mirror. Tell your mate the reason it's up there is because you have to remember it. It will change your mate's life as well, just because he or she has to look at it.

• Make a decision for yourself that no matter what it takes, you are not going to buy into the old point of view. You're not going to continue to live a diminished life.

• Create every day of your life as a celebration. Every morning say, *Just for today, my life will be a celebration,* and watch for the new possibilities that will show up.

A NOTE TO READERS

The information presented in this book is actually just a small taste of what Access has to offer. There is a whole universe of Access processes and classes. If there are places where you can't get things to work in your life the way you know they ought to, you might be interested in attending an Access class or locating an Access facilitator who can work with you to give you greater clarity about issues you can't overcome. Access processes are done with a trained facilitator, and are based on the energy of you and the person you're working with.

For more information, visit:
www.AccessConsciousness.com

GLOSSARY

Bars

The bars are a hands-on Access process that involves a light touch upon the head to contact points that correspond to different aspects of one's life. There are points for joy, sadness, body and sexuality, awareness, kindness, gratitude, peace and calm. There is even a money bar. These points are called bars because they run from one side of the head to the other.

Be

In this book, the word be is sometimes used to refer to you, the infinite being you truly be, as opposed to a contrived point of view about who you think you are.

Clearing Statement (POD/POC)

The clearing statement we use in Access is: Right and wrong, good and bad, POD, POC, all nine, shorts, boys and beyonds.™

Right and wrong, good and bad is shorthand for: What's good, perfect and correct about this? What's wrong, mean, vicious, terrible, bad and awful about this? What's right and wrong, good and bad?

POC is the point of creation of the thoughts, feelings and emotions immediately preceding whatever you decided.

POD is the point of destruction immediately preceding whatever you decided. It's like pulling the bottom card out of a house of cards. The whole thing falls down.

All nine stands for nine layers of crap that were taken out. You know that somewhere in those nine layers, there's got to be a pony because you couldn't put that much shit in one place without having a pony in there. It's shit that you're generating yourself, which is the bad part.

Shorts is the short version of: What's meaningful about this? What's meaningless about this? What's the punishment for this? What's the reward for this?

Boys stands for nucleated spheres. Have you ever seen one of those kids' bubble pipes? Blow here and you create a mass of bubbles. You pop one bubble and the other bubbles fill in the space

Beyonds are feelings or sensations you get that stop your heart, stop your breath, or stop your willingness to look at possibilities. It's like when your business is in the red and you get another final notice and you say argh! You weren't expecting that right now.

Sometimes, instead of saying "use the clearing statement," we just say, "POD and POC it."

OTHER BOOKS

The Place
By Gary M. Douglas

As Jake Rayne travels through Idaho in his classic 57 Thunderbird, a devastating accident is the catalyst for a journey he isn't expecting. Alone in the deep forest, with his body shattered and broken, Jake calls out for help. The help that finds him changes not only his life but his whole reality. Jake is opened up to the awareness of possibilities; possibilities that we have always known should be but that have not yet shown up. A Barnes and Noble Best Seller.

Being You, Changing the World
By Dr. Dain Heer

Have you always known that something COMPLETELY DIFFERENT is possible? What if you had a handbook for infinite possibilities and dynamic change to guide you? With tools and processes that actually worked and invited you to a completely different way of being? For you? And the world?

Divorceless Relationships
By Gary M. Douglas

What if you don't have to divorce you in order to create an intimate relationship? This book contains tools, exercises and processes you can use so you do not have to give up any part of yourself in a relationship.

Magic. You are it. Be it.
By Gary M. Douglas & Dr. Dain Heer

Magic is about the fun of having the things you desire. The real magic is the ability to have the joy that life can be. In this book you are presented tools & points of view that you can use to create consciousness and magic—and change your life in ways you may not even be able to imagine.

Talk to the Animals
By Gary M. Douglas & Dr. Dain Heer

Did you know that every animal, every plant, every structure on this planet has consciousness and desires to gift to you? Animals have a tremendous amount of information and amazing gifts they can give to us if we are willing to receive them.

Sex is Not a Four Letter Word but Relationship Often Times Is
By Gary M. Douglas & Dr. Dain Heer

Funny , frank, and delightfully irreverent, this book offers readers an entirely fresh view of how to create great intimacy and exceptional sex. What if you could stop guessing—and find out what REALLY works?

Right Riches for You!
By Gary M. Douglas & Dr. Dain Heer

What if generating money and having money were fun and joyful? What if, in having fun and joy with money, you receive more of it? What would that be like? Money follows joy; joy does not follow money. As seen on Lifetime Television's Balancing Act Show.

ABOUT THE AUTHORS

Gary M. Douglas

The illustrious best-selling author and international speaker, Gary Douglas, pioneered a set of transformational life changing tools and processes known as Access Consciousness® over 20 years ago. These cutting edge tools have transformed the lives of thousands of people all over the world. In fact, his work has spread to 47 countries, with 2,000 trained facilitators worldwide. Simple but so effective, the tools facilitate people of all ages and backgrounds to help remove limitations holding them back from a full life.

Gary was born in Midwest USA and raised in San Diego, California. Although he came from a *"normal"* middle class family, he was fascinated from an early age with the human psyche and this interest grew into a desire to assist people to *"know what they know"* and expand into more awareness, joy and abundance. These pragmatic tools he has developed are not only being used by celebrities, corporates and teachers but also by health professionals (psychologists, chiropractors, naturopaths) to improve the health & wellbeing of their clients.

Prior to creating Access Consciousness® Gary Douglas was a successful realtor in Santa Barbara, California and also completed a psychology degree. Although he attained material wealth and was regarded as *"successful,"* his life began to lack meaning and so he began his search to find a new way forward- one that would create change in the world and in people's lives.

Gary is the author of 8 books including the best selling novel *"The Place."* He describes the inspiration behind the writing, *"I wanted to explore the possibilities for how life could be. To allow people to know there actually is no necessity to live with the ageing, insanity, stupidity, intrigue, violence, craziness, trauma and drama we live with, as though we have no choice. "The Place" is about people knowing that all things are possible. Choice is the source of creation. What if our choices can be changed in an instant? What if we could make choice more real than the decisions and stuck points we buy as real?"*

Gary has an incredible level of awareness and care for all living things, *"I would like people be more aware and more conscious and to realize we need to be stewards of the earth not users and abusers of the earth. If we start to see the possibilities of what we have available to us, instead of trying to create our piece of the pie, we could create a different world."*

A vibrant 70-year-old grandfather (*who is almost "ageless"*) with a very different view on life, Gary believes we are here to express our uniqueness and experience the ease and joy of living. He continues to inspire others, teaching across the world and making a massive contribution to the planet. He openly proclaims that for him, *"life is just beginning."*

Gary also has a wide range of personal and other business interests. These include: a passion for antiques (*Gary established "The Antique Guild" in Brisbane, Australia in 2012*) riding spirited stallions and breeding Costarricense De Paso horses, and an eco retreat in Costa Rica set to open in 2014.

To find out more, please visit:
www.GaryMDouglas.com
www.AccessConsciousness.com
www.Costarricense-Paso.com

Dr. Dain Heer

Dr. Dain Heer is an international speaker, author and facilitator of advanced Access Consciousness® workshops worldwide. His unique and transforming points of view on bodies, money, future, sex and relationships transcend everything currently being taught.

Dr. Heer invites and inspires people to greater conscious awareness from total allowance, caring, humor and a deep inner knowing.

Dr. Heer started work as a Network Chiropractor back in 2000 in California, USA. He came across Access Consciousness® at a point in his life when he was deeply unhappy and even planning suicide.

When none of the other modalities and techniques Dr. Heer had been studying were giving him lasting results or change, Access Consciousness® changed everything for him and his life began to expand and grow with more ease and speed than even he could have imagined possible.

Dr. Heer now travels the world facilitating classes and has developed a unique energy process for change for individuals and groups, called The Energetic Synthesis of Being. He has a completely different approach to healing by teaching people to tap into and recognize their own abilities and knowing. The energetic transformation possible is fast—and truly dynamic.

To find out more, please visit:
www.DrDainHeer.com
www.BeingYouChangingTheWorld.com
www.BeingYouClass.com

ABOUT ACCESS CONSCIOUSNESS®

Access Consciousness® is an energy transformation program which links seasoned wisdom, ancient knowledge and channeled energies with highly contemporary motivational tools. Its purpose is to set you free by giving you access to your truest, highest self.

The purpose of Access is to create a world of consciousness and oneness. Consciousness includes everything and judges nothing. It is our target to facilitate you to the point where you receive awareness of everything with no judgment of anything. If you have no judgment of anything, then you get to look at everything for what it is, not for what you want it to be, not for what it ought to be, but just for what it is.

Consciousness is the ability to be present in your life in every moment, without judgment of you or anyone else. It is the ability to receive everything, reject nothing, and create everything you desire in life-greater than what you currently have, and more than what you can imagine.

What if you were willing to nurture and care for you?

What if you would open the doors to being everything you have decided it is not possible to be?

What would it take for you to realize how crucial you are to the possibilities of the world?

The information, tools and techniques presented in this book are just a small taste of what Access Consciousness® has to offer. There is a whole Universe of processes and classes.

If there are places where you can't get things in your life to work the way you know they ought to, then you might be interested in attended an Access Consciousness® class, workshop or locating a facilitator. They can work with you to give you greater clarity about issues you haven't yet overcome.

Access Consciousness® processes are done with a trained facilitator, and are based on the energy of you and the person you're working with.

Come and explore more at:
www.AccessConsciousness.com

ACCESS SEMINARS & CLASSES

If you liked what you read in this book and are interested in attended Access seminars, workshops or classes, then for a very different point of view, read-on and sample a taste of what is available.

Access Bars (One Day)

Facilitated by Certified Access Bars Facilitators worldwide, Bars is one of the foundational tools of Access. In this one day class, you will learn a hands-on energetic process, which you will gift and receive during the class. The Access Bars are 32 points on the head that when lightly touched clear all of the limitations you have about different areas of your life and body. This areas include money, aging, body, sexuality, joy, sadness, healing, creativity, awareness and control plus many more. What would it be like to have more freedom is all of these areas? In this one day class you will learn the basic tools of Access Consciousness® and receive and gift 2 Access Bars sessions. At worst it will feel like a great massage and at best your whole life will change!

Prerequisites: None
Facilitied by Certified Access Facilitators Worldwide

Access Foundation (Two Day)

This two day class is about giving you the space to look at your life as a different possibility. Unlock your limitations about emobdiment, finances, success, relationships, family, YOU and your capacities, and much more! Step into greater possibilities for having everything you truly desire in life as you learn tools and questions to change anything that's not working for you.

Prerequisites: Access Bars
Facilitated by Certified Access Facilitators Worldwide

Access, Level 1 (Two Day)

This is a two day class that shows you how to be more conscious in every area of your life and gives you practical tools that allow you to continue expanding this in your day-to-day! Create a phenomenal life filled with magic, joy and ease and clear your limitations about what is truly available for you. Discover the 5 Elements of Intimacy, create energy flows, start laughing and celebrating living and practice a hands-on body process that has created miraculous results all over the world!

Prerequisites: Access Foundation
Facilitated Exclusively by Gary M. Douglas and Dr. Dain Heer

Access, Levels 2 & 3 (Four Day)

Having completed Level I and opened up to more awareness of you, you start to have more choice in life and become aware of what choice truly is. This four day class covers a huge range of areas including the joy of business, living life for the fun of it, no fear, courage and leadership, changing the molecular structure of things, creating your body and your sexual reality, and how to stop holding on to what you want to get rid of! Is it time to start receiving the change you've been asking for?

Prerequisites: Access Bars, Foundation, and Level I
Facilitated Exclusively by Gary M. Douglas and Dr. Dain Heer

The Energetic Synthesis of Being - ESB (Three Day)

This three day class is a unique way of working with energy, groups of people and their bodies simultaneously, created and facilitated by Dr. Dain Heer. During this class, your being, your body and the earth are invited to energetically snythesize in a way that creates a more conscious life and a more conscious planet. You begin to access and be energies you never knew were available. By being these energies, by being you, you change everything; the planet, your life and everyone you come into contact with. What else is possible then?

Prerequisites: Access Bars, Foundation and Level I, II, & III
Facilitated Exclusively by Dr. Dain Heer

Access Body Class (Two Day)

During this two day class you will learn verbal processes and hands on bodywork that unlock the tension, resistance, and dis-ease of the body. Do you have a talent and ability to work with bodies that you haven't yet unlocked? Are you a body worker (massage therapist, chiropractor, medical doctor, nurse) looking for a way to enhance the healing you can do for your clients? Come play with us and begin to explore how to communicate and relate to bodies, including yours, in a whole new way.

Prerequisites: Access Bars
Facilitated by Access Body Class Facilitators Worldwide.

CONNECT WITH ACCESS ONLINE

www.AccessConciousness.com
www.GaryMDouglas.com
www.DrDainHeer.com
www.BeingYouChangingtheWorld.com

www.YouTube.com/drdainheer
www.Facebook.com/drdainheer
www.Twitter.com/drdainheer

www.Facebook.com/accessconsciousness
www.RightRecoveryForYou.com
www.AccessTrueKnowledge.com

CPSIA information can be obtained
at www.ICGtesting.com
Printed in the USA
FSOW02n1218250116
15985FS